Andre Dubus

Tributes

Andre Dubus

Tributes

Donald Anderson
Editor

Xavier Review Press
New Orleans
2001

Contents

Critical Studies

Preface

The Colonel's Wife

25 May 1992
Memorial Day — starting
3rd draft

The retired Marine colonel had
two broken legs, both in casts from the
soles of his feet to the tops of his thighs.
His name was Robert ~~James~~ Townsend;
he was a tall and broad-shouldered man
with black hair and a graying moustache.
In the hospital in Boston he had five
operations; neither leg was healed enough
to bear his weight, he had rods in
both femurs and his right tibia,
and now at home he was fourteen
in the living room on a hospital bed
whose ends he could raise and
lower, to evade pain. The bed was
narrow, and his golden-haired wife,
Lydia, slept upstairs.

"The Colonel's Wife"
2nd draft

Andre Dubus

Thomas Bonner, Jr.

Andre Dubus and His Worlds

Why writers come from areas of the country not dominated by blocks and blocks of publishers is always a mystery. Mississippi writers, for instance, exist in such abundance as to cause critics and scholars to make persistent inquiries into the phenomenon. How do we explain William Faulkner and Eudora Welty, whose times intersected there? Even less explainable is that Mississippi's cities of literary influence have been Memphis and New Orleans, both out-of-state. Mississippi's neighboring state of Louisiana has a similar long history of producing writers as well as sustaining and inspiring visiting ones. Walker Percy emigrated from Greenville, Mississippi to New Orleans and then Covington, Louisiana. Earlier Sherwood Anderson had worked and lived above Jackson Square in New Orleans. Much earlier, George Washington Cable, a native of New Orleans, wrote *The Grandissimes*, which journeys through the French, Spanish, Americans, and Africans at the time of the Louisiana Purchase.

Louisiana has at least three broad cultures: the Anglo-Saxon in the North, the Creole in New Orleans and Natchitoches, and the Acadian, these days better known as *Cajun*, in the southern and southwestern part of the state. The African-American culture influences all regions of both Mississippi and Louisiana. From this ethnic and cultural milieu comes Andre Dubus, born and schooled in Lafayette, the heart of the Cajun country. If small town life was celebrated and explored in American letters before World War II, Andre's life in Louisiana, on the margins of the nation, reflected an extension of that world. It was a town dominated by its Roman Catholic cathedral, touched by the banks of the Vermillion River, bordered by fields of rice, and influenced by the machinery of the oil industry, and entertained by minor league baseball and the folk music of the region. Tempered by the tolerance of its French culture and its university, the city generated an openness that affected

Andre's perspectives on himself and other people.

When he attended McNeese State University in Lake Charles, west of Lafayette and near the border with Texas, he began slowly to find himself as a writer. His journalistic efforts in the college paper reflected the conservatism of a person of his familial, religious, and communal origins. His participation in the Louisiana College Writers' Society advanced the scope of his writing to include literature. When he left Louisiana for the United States Marine Corps, he brought with him the seeds of being a writer: an intensely lived youth and a powerful memory. His new experiences were not lost as his novel *The Lieutenant*—the thesis for his graduate work at the University of Iowa Writers' Workshop—and several of his stories demonstrate.

Like a number of Southern writers, Dubus left the region to live and work. He joined the ranks of Ernest Gaines, Robert Morgan, Truman Capote, John Barth, A.R. Ammons, and others whose expatriate lives led them into a new mix of characters and places but whose distance from the land of their rearing never insinuated itself between the power of setting and the development of characters. We can be amused at Barry Hannah's observation in *Boomerang*: "All the generations of wonderful dead guys behind us. All the Confederate dead and the Union dead planted in the soil near us. All of Faulkner the great. Christ, there's barely room for the living down here." In his Haverhill, Massachusetts home, Dubus wrote stories that drew on the place and region of his abode, but his characters always seemed to spring from the earth in which he planted them. The presence and necessity of the soil, the earth, never left him, but in the free space of New England he did shake from his boots any southern clichés that might have stuck.

His characters, rooted in place and experience, come from a world of hard work. Possessing the ragged scars and dark bruises of conflict, they are kin to antecedent characters drawn by William and John Faulkner and Erskine Caldwell. Like Dubus himself, his characters are distinct. When Larry Brown in "A Late Start" wrote of his interest in "how people bear up under monstrous calamity, all the terrible things that can befall them, war, poverty, desperation," he could have been writing about Dubus and his characters, especially in the aftermath of his debilitating and life changing accident.

In this volume we are celebrating the contributions of a man's life to the world of letters. Dubus, despite and perhaps because of troubling shadows and raging conflicts within himself, still had enough grace to serve as a sacred vessel ministering to readers, writers, and those near to him. His son Andre III, a notable writer himself, gives us a small and intimate portrait of the man and writer. His sister Kathryn Dubus recalls Andre's youth and family life as his cousin James Lee Burke tells us about Andre's love of baseball and his ingrained generosity. Although in his professional writing life, Andre dropped the French spelling of his first name, his sister, Kathryn, asked that we use the French form of her brother's name in her essay "Brother André." "It's how we spelled his name growing up," she explained in a telephone conversation. "It's how Daddy's name is spelled on his grave. It's how I spelled it when I wrote to Brother André, and, by the way, it's how I spell young André's name when I write to him." Joe Massa, a schoolmate and later a journalist, remembers Andre's soccer playing and Catholicism in Lafayette. Father Patrick Samway, S.J., who interviewed Dubus for *Xavier Review* in 1988, narrates Dubus' complex personal and literary life and offers a meditation on that life, one in which "he knew what he wanted to do, but he had no map to get him there." Remembering his and Andre's tumultuous first meeting, Tobias Wolff reflects on the varied ingredients of Andre's personality and character distilling themselves into a rich fiction. In the end Wolff moves readers to consider his own loss and the losses of the writers in this volume occasioned by Andre's now empty wheelchair.

The caption to a picture beginning a commemoration of Dubus in *StoryQuarterly 35*, "*well met, well loved, well missed,*" extends to the reflections of the writers, editors, and publishers who have contributed to this volume. What is startling about Dubus is that despite his being long read by a narrow range of readers, he and his work have touched and intersected with the lives of so many workers in the vineyard of literary culture that those writing here represent the blooms and fruit of American writing today.

Lee K. Abbott observes of Dubus that he "seemed to know the why of our what." Remembering Dubus' essay "On Charon's Wharf," Marilyn Abildskov quotes a sentence that touched a moment in her life: "*When you believe you no longer love, you no longer do.*" The editor of this volume, Donald Anderson, encountered Dubus' writing when he was in M.F.A. study at Cornell University during which time *Epoch* was publishing Dubus' work and later when Anderson himself published Dubus in *War, Literature & the Arts*. Doris Betts comments on the women who frequently surrounded Andre and observes, "The women in both his life and on his pages were not always admirers, even lovers." When Dubus went to Colgate University to read for the first time "A Father's Story," Frederick Busch remembers the impact on a particular woman in the audience. Alan Cheuse, whose observations were first broadcast on PBS's "All Things Considered," notes that after Dubus became disabled, "he displayed honesty, and ferocity and directness but not a trace of self-pity." David Godine, Andre's long time publisher, points out the dichotomy between the sentimentality that was part of Dubus' life and its consistent omission in his fiction. William B. Goodman, Dubus' editor at Godine, emphasizes—in the context of his passion for short fiction—the importance Dubus placed on "oral reality" as part of the process of composing.

This epic catalog of tributes continues as M.M.M. Hayes remembers Dubus' seeing himself as a "workingman" and his emphasizing the power that comes when a writer loves his characters. Kacey Kowars shows us consoling correspondence that Dubus had written him during a difficult period in Kowars' life. Charles E. May admires Andre's loyalty to the short story in the face of publishers' demands for novels. Seeing Dubus as "a writer who valued memory and the spiritual quality of ordinary experience," James McConkey marvels on his essay "Under the Lights." As several contributors to this volume do, Kai Maristed recalls the events of the Thursday workshops, and notes that while Dubus "was not always particularly kind," he was generous in that "he never held back." Never having met Dubus, James Hughes Meredith finds in his writing a shared experience in suffering, sacrifice, and sacrament—questions and issues inherent in a Roman Catholic life. Chris Offutt remembers first reading Dubus while standing in the aisle of a bookstore. Meeting Dubus at a reading in Syracuse when he was a student, Robert Olmstead describes how "He and I talked about the beauty of having daughters." Tim Parrish narrates his driving Dubus to a reading in Baton Rouge, Louisiana, and muses on Andre's encouragement when Parrish was considering the writing program at the University of Alabama. A member of Dubus' gratis writing workshop in Haverhill, Massachusetts, Richard Ravin paints an image of a robust and vulnerable Andre on one of those Thursday nights. Darrell Spencer looks into Dubus when he observes, "I bet he was not a man who was at peace except for a minute here and there, say, when Liv Ullmann rested her hand on his shoulder" [after the accident]. Citing the power of friendship and shared experience, Dubus' agent Philip G. Spitzer remarks on the writer's standing by his "conviction" in his loyalty to David Godine, who first published him and in his often selfless concern for the success of writers he admired. Lara JK Wilson observes Dubus' finding "the knot, the cell of concern" after a problematic workshop reading and then leaving the writer "with the inspiration, the will to write." In defending the publication of Dubus' "If They Knew Yvonne," Robley Wilson takes pride in its being one of the *Best American Short Stories of 1970*, and prompted by his affection for "A Father's Story," which he sees as "a nearly perfect exemplar of his work: the war between two kinds of conscience, two kinds of obligation, two loyalties—the one secular, the other religious."

Also among these remembrances, these tributes, are those from *StoryQuarterly 35*: Thomas E. Kennedy's account of how he was inspired to write *Andre Dubus: A Study of the Short Fiction*, Nancy Zafris' response to Dubus' selecting her story for *Black Warrior Review*'s annual best short story award, and Amy Schildhouse Greenberg's memory of Dubus as a teacher of writing and life.

The spring of 2001 brought other kinds of recognition for Dubus. Peggy Rambach explored her married life with Dubus in the novel *Fighting Gravity* (Steerforth Press) making him a subject as well as a writer. Babineau, the character based on Dubus, resembles much of what people have come to know about the writer, as he and Ellie (modeled on Rambach) amid their imperfection see "their earthly task to become better people than the ones they'd been before and thus set an example for all, of courage, nobility, and enduring love." Furthermore, scholars and critics gathered in Baltimore, Maryland for the first conference devoted to Dubus and his writing. The greatest literary tribute, however, is his son Andre III's success as a writer and as a writer who shares his father's sensibilities of the blue-collar world.

In addition to conceiving of this volume as an honor for Andre Dubus and his writing, we also saw this effort as a means of encouraging its further consideration by readers and scholars. Accordingly, Brian Hanley examines the critical reception of Dubus' fiction and essays; Thomas G. Bowie, Jr. offers a close consideration of Andre's literary nonfiction; and Will Hochman explores the "poetry" of Dubus' prose. To present an account of the images of himself that Dubus offered in his interviews, Ross Gresham provides a description and an analysis of more than twenty from 1981 through 1999. Finally, Robert E. Skinner presents a descriptive bibliography of Dubus' short fiction, essays—with first appearances of both in periodicals—and books, along with notes on conditions and eccentricities associated with their publishing.

Andre Dubus and his writings have traveled far from his native Louisiana. His subsequent experiences in the northeast and on the seas as a Marine and in the Midwest as a graduate student have become attributes to a life and a body of writing that grew from his early years in the Acadian country of Louisiana and in the teachings of his Church. In "Witness," Dubus' final essay in *Meditations from a Movable Chair*, his last sentence reads, "Today the light came: *I am here*." It was not an end but a beginning, for him, for all of us, and his many readers to come.

Thomas Bonner, Jr. is editor of *Xavier Review* Press and the journal *Xavier Review*. He has books on William Faulkner, Kate Chopin, and southern poetry and fiction, as well as a chapbook on Edgar Allan Poe and articles, stories, essays, and poems in many periodicals. He is Distinguished Visiting Professor at the United States Air Force Academy and Endowed Professor of English at Xavier University of Louisiana.

Foreword

He refused to eat in bed for that made him feel he was still in the hospital; so at mealtimes Lydia helped him onto the wheelchair. He raised the bed till he was upright, she handed him a short board with bevelled ends, and he pushed one end under his ~~butt~~ rump and rested the other on the chair. Then she held his legs while he worked himself across the board. He wore cotton gym shorts and tee shirts.

⟵ Before the horse fell on him, he and Lydia had eaten breakfast and lunch at the kitchen table. He could not go there now. He could not wheel through the door from the dining room to the kitchen; then his long legs, held ~~by~~ by legrests ~~that~~ straight out in front of him, were blocked by a counter, and at his

"The Colonel's Wife"
2nd draft

Andre Dubus

Andre Dubus III

My Father, Andre Dubus

From 1964 to 1966, my family lived in Iowa City on a brick street on a hill with only two other houses on it. My father was a graduate student at the University of Iowa, though I didn't know this at the time; I was five or six years old, and all I knew was that we didn't live on a military base anymore and that my father was no longer a captain in the Marines, and he'd let his hair grow out long enough you could actually see some on his head, thick and brown. He'd grown a moustache, too.

Though I didn't have words for it, I'd never seem him happier; he laughed often and loudly; he hugged and kissed our mother at every turn; at night before bed, he'd sit me, my brother, and two sisters down at the kitchen table or on the couch out in the living room and he'd tell us stories he made up himself—adventure stories where the hero and heroine were Indians defending their families and their people from the white man. One of them was named Running Blue Ice Water, a kind and brave warrior who lingered in my imagination long after we'd been tucked in upstairs in a large room all four of us children shared.

We didn't own a television then, but my mother and father probably had a record player because there would be jazz playing on the nights they had parties, loud parties with a lot of loud grownup noise. In our bedroom floor was an air vent that overlooked the living room, and sometimes on party nights we kids would huddle around it and spy on our mother and father and their friends below, watch them dance and drink and argue and laugh, the men always louder than the women, their cigarette smoke curling up through the grate into our faces. I remember hearing a lot of dirty words then but also ones like *story*, *novel*, and *poem*. *Chekhov* and *Hemingway*. *Art* and *death*.

In the morning we'd be up long before our parents. We'd get our cereal and poke around in the party ruins, the table and floors of our small house littered with empty beer bottles, crushed potato chips, overflowing ashtrays, half the butts brushed with lipstick. If there was anything left in a glass, and if there weren't a cigarette floating in it, my sister Suzanne and I would take a few sips because we liked the taste of watered-down whiskey or gin. Once we found a carrot cake in the living room. Its sides were covered with white frosting, but the middle was nothing but a mashed crater. I remembered the cake from the night before, a mouth-watering three layer with frosted writing on the top. I asked my mother who it was for and she said it was for one of their friends who'd just sold his novel to a publisher; they were going to celebrate. I don't know if I asked her what a novel was then, or a publisher, but I'm sure I didn't really know. And now the cake was unrecognizable, and when my mother came down that morning looking young and beautiful, probably in shorts and one of my father's shirts, smoking a cigarette, only twenty-five or six then, I asked her what had happened to the cake. She dug her finger into the frosting, then smiled at me. "Just your father and his crazy writer friends, honey." I wasn't sure if that meant he was a crazy writer too, but I knew there was a black wooden desk in the front room overlooking our yard, and Dad would go there everyday and shut the door and we had to be quiet or go play outside, so I thought maybe he *was* one.

It was another party at our house that confirmed it for me, though, one that began with jazz on the record player, a platter of cucumbers and carrots and horseradish dip on the kitchen table, glasses set out on the counter, and in his front room on the big desk were two lit candles on either side of something rectangle and about two or three inches high covered with a black cloth. As my father's friends showed up one or two couples at a time, he'd walk them into this room with a drink or bottle of beer in his hand, and he'd point at what he told them was the failed novel he was holding a funeral for. He'd laugh and they'd laugh and one of his writer friends would put his hand on his shoulder and squeeze, both of them looking suddenly pained and quite serious, and I knew then my father was a writer too.

When his first book was published in 1967, his novel *The Lieutenant*, we were living in New Hampshire in a rented cottage in the woods. It was small, with only three downstairs rooms—the kitchen, the living room, and the den where our father would go and shut the door and we'd play in the woods while he smoked a pipe and drank iced tea and wrote. When he was done two or three hours later, he looked tired and spent but strangely calm and happy. I assumed everyone's fathers did this, closed themselves off in a quiet room and tried to write good stories.

A year or so after my father's novel was published, Burt Lancaster called our house and then Dad was flown to a place called Hollywood. Days or weeks later, my mother, brother, two sisters, and I met him at Logan Airport in Boston. He got off the plane looking tanned and relaxed, his eyes filling up as he hugged us all. I was eight or nine years old, my brother a year younger, and in the Men's Room, after using those strange stand-up toilets and washing our hands, Pop took out his wallet and handed both of us a one hundred dollar bill to go show our mother. There was the feeling something big was happening to our whole family, something big and good; none of us, including my mother, had ever seen a one hundred dollar bill before, and my father had written a book somebody wanted to make into a movie. For a few months, my mother and father didn't have to worry about getting all the bills paid on time; he just had to write something called a screenplay. So, back home, he went into that quiet room with his pipe and iced tea, and he wrote those pages he'd been paid to write, but he didn't look so happy anymore doing it; now he looked to me like a man forced to carry a weight he wasn't sure how to get out from under.

But that wasn't the only thing troubling him or my mother; we owned a TV now, a black and white on which nightly were pictures of soldiers being dragged through tall grass beaten down by helicopter blades. One newscast showed the bodies of a dozen Marines all shot or stabbed after they were already dead, and I watched my father cry on the couch for these men he called boys. He had just grown a beard, and he looked to me then like a man from an earlier time. This was also the year Martin Luther King, Jr. and Robert Kennedy were shot just months apart, there were riots at the democratic convention in Chicago, and the parties my parents threw became more serious with less laughing and more loud talk. This was the year their marriage ended and Burt Lancaster called back to say they'd never be able to shoot this movie, a story set on an aircraft carrier when all the carriers were in Southeast Asia, and it'd be too expensive to build one as a set; it seemed like the only bit of good news my father got that year. He didn't have to work on the screenplay anymore and he could go back to the fiction he'd never really left. He was thirty-two years old and was reading a lot of Anton Chekhov then, the writer who would become his mentor. When I was grown, he told me he finished reading Chekhov's "The Duel" one afternoon in that cottage in the woods, went straight into his den, threw away the novel-length story he'd been working on for months, and told himself it was time he taught himself to *write*. He believed the short story to be the higher form, and even though he knew quite well that publishers were far more interested in the more "commercial" novel, he never wrote another one.

When I began reading my father's work for the first time, I was fifteen or sixteen years old. I was visiting his mother in Lake Charles, Louisiana, and she put *The Lieutenant* into my hands and told me to go read it. I was already a reader and was happy to do it, though my expectations were not high because my dad wrote it and how good could my own father's book be? I'd read some Steinbeck and Hemingway, some Faulkner, Katherine Anne Porter, and J.D. Salinger. I loved these writers and couldn't imagine them as anything *but* writers—certainly not as fathers or mothers, husbands or wives. How could you be that and a great writer? So I was not expecting greatness as I lay on my lovely grandmother's couch in her air-conditioned house in the heat of a Louisiana summer, opened my father's book, and read the first line which pulled me to the next and the next to four hours later and the very end of the novel; my grandmother's living room had turned gold with the light of early evening, the house smelled of crawfish étouffée and homemade bread, and inside me was my father's glorious book and all its vivid images and tastes and smells, but more; I felt the souls of the people in that book, and because I felt their souls, I felt my father's soul more, too, the same way I'd felt Steinbeck's, Hemingway's, and the rest. And I even felt my own soul, something inside of me and outside of me all at once. Which meant my father was a great writer, too? Yes, I told myself, he's one, too.

A few years later, on a cold gray day back in New England, I read his short story, "Killings." When I finished I had to leave my house and go for a walk. This story of such loss and hope and more loss left me feeling so much that I could not keep my body still; I had to move just so I wouldn't be physically overwhelmed by my grief and awe and even joy. It was the same way I'd felt after reading Steinbeck's *The Grapes of Wrath* a year earlier, a 500-page novel with a dozen major characters that begins in dust bowl Oklahoma and ends in the flooded vineyards of California; but my father had done the same thing with an eighteen-page short story set in a small New England town!

Over the years, he began to give us typed copies of his stories as soon as he finished them. Throughout his thirties and forties, he wrote three stories a year every year, though quite a few took him longer to write; his story "Waiting" took him fourteen months. At one point in its composition, it was over a hundred pages long. When he finally finished it, it was seven pages and was published in *The Paris Review*. I read it standing in a bookstore aisle in Austin, Texas, where I was a college student, this story of a young widow getting older alone. Again, I could feel her soul and her creator's soul—my father—and my soul, too. I left the bookstore and stepped into the bright Texas heat feeling as if I'd just grown somehow. I called him that night back in Massachusetts to tell him how much I liked his new story, and that's when he told me how long it had taken and how many pages he had to write to find those seven.

"Find?"

"Yep. I never know what I'm doing. I trust the story and God to tell me."

"God?"

"Oh yes, son. God."

A couple of years later, I lay in bed on a Sunday morning and read in manuscript "A Father's Story," one of his absolute finest works that ends with the protagonist, Luke Ripley, having a conversation with God. Who else but my devout, gifted, hard-working father would even *try* to pull off something like that? And, once again, here it came, this opening up inside me, a revealing and merging of soul and spirit that only high art can achieve. And it happened—and happens—with all his stories, these complicated human lives he wrote about—men, women, and children caught up in some kind of broken web they will either endure and prevail over, or not.

Slowly his work began to be read more widely. More and more reviewers used the word "master" when writing about him and his fiction. And of course they were right, though not once did I ever hear him use that word himself. Once, over a beer on his deck, I told him I thought he was one of the best writers in the country, and he said, "Well, you just haven't read enough then." And he smiled and slapped my leg.

He never kept reviews; he threw away not only the rare bad ones but the wonderful ones too, those that called him a master and even compared him to the great Russian writers. He'd read them once, then throw them away, convinced good news was as distracting and potentially harmful to the artist as the bad.

I keep seeing him as I knew him all through his thirties and forties, the twenty-year period when he wrote and published the bulk of his life's work. Until he and his wife bought a house when he turned fifty, he always lived in cheap campus housing at Bradford College where he taught, or in small rented apartments full of books and old jazz records, his barbells and weight bench, his desk beside a bookshelf overflowing with all of his publications, most of them in literary quarterlies he preferred to have his work appear in; those years he drove used cars—old Fords and Chevys. He went to Mass daily and wrote and went for a run. On his birthday in August, he and I used to run together, an eleven-mile route over a hilly dirt road in the trees along the water, both of us sweating and breathing hard, running side by side, talking about whatever came up: family and friends, the president and his policies, books we were reading, women and men, workout routines, the beer and tequila we were going to drink when the sun went down. And as loud and raucous as he could be on those nights, I never lost sight of the man who lived daily so steadfastly in service to his art, which is, it seems to me, an intrinsically humble way to live, and passionate too.

After he got run over in the summer of 1986, after seven weeks of hospitalization and ten operations that ended with the amputation of his left leg, after months of painful physical therapy, he lay on his bed with his remaining but useless leg propped on pillows, and he wrote his short story, "The Curse." I was there the day he finished it and saw him weep with joy because he thought he'd lost whatever it is that gives writers stories to tell, that it had somehow been knocked out of him permanently that summer night he'd been run over by a car at 58 miles an hour. But it was back, and he knew it, and when we all read it, we knew it too.

A few years later, he had a mild heart attack and was back in the hospital. I went to visit him there one night after work, but his room was empty, and this scared me because he'd had a heart attack and an empty room could only mean one thing; I walked up and down the halls looking for him, my own heart knocking against my ribs. I turned a corner and there he was in the doorway of a small bathroom, sitting in his wheelchair with his back to the hallway. The door was propped against his left wheel. I thought maybe he was washing his hands, but as I got closer I could see over his shoulder the notebook propped against the sink, his moving hand with the pen in it. There was a sheen of sweat on his forehead, and his green Johnny looked too small for him. I didn't want to disturb him, and I started to back away, but he turned and looked up at me. "Hey, man. Too many people going in and out of that room; I had to find someplace to *write*."

I kissed the top of his balding head and told him I'd catch him later.

After I left, he finished that story in one sitting and one draft. It was "Love Song," the most lyrical piece in what would become his last book of fiction, *Dancing After Hours*.

His heart gave out in the shower at his house in Haverhill, Massachusetts on February 24, 1999 at age 62. My brother Jeb and I built his coffin out of pine fastened with glue and dowels. My wife, Fontaine, and my mother lined the inside with tan satin sheets from his bed. For the funeral, we dressed him in the clothes he had laid out for himself—a dark pullover shirt, sweat pants, a sock, and the purple bandana he used to tie the empty pant leg folded to his stump. In April, when the ground had thawed, Jeb and I, and our good friend, Bill Cantwell, dug Dad's grave with shovels and a pick, and we buried him on Fenway Park's opening day. A Catholic priest was there, and seven Marines in dress blues and white gloves who gave him a twenty-one gun salute, and a lone bagpiper played "Amazing Grace," walking off into the cemetery until we couldn't hear or see him anymore.

A few weeks later, I drove to my father's house and let myself in. I walked down the dark hallway, the walls still painted in the green, orange, and blue strokes of my younger sisters. In his bedroom I turned on the overhead light. There were some half-packed cardboard boxes on his bed. On the wall above it, between two dark windows, was the framed faded photograph of him in uniform with his Marine Corps platoon thirty-five years earlier. The wall beyond his headboard was still nothing but floor to ceiling shelves full of books. At the foot of his bed was the bench where he used to do Roman Chair situps, (which he could only do once he'd transferred there from his wheelchair then used his leather weight belt to tie his crushed leg and stump to the bench itself). On the opposite wall over a low bookshelf hung eight or ten hats: Australian Akubras, a Stetson, a Drill Instructor's head cover, a straw Panama, and two faded Red Sox caps.

I pushed a box aside and sat on his bed, looked at his plywood desk he had me build that was wide and low enough for the wheelchair that now sat under it. On his desk were some new notebooks he'd bought and had planned to fill; there was the Bowie knife my sister and I had given him he'd used as a paperweight; there was a dirty ashtray, a wooden crucifix, photographs of my younger sisters, and stacks of books, mainly literary quarterlies. On top was a cloth-bound journal. I picked it up and opened it. It was full of my father's graceful penmanship in ink. On each page were six or seven dates and what he'd written next to them: that day's workout (Roman Chair situps, shadow boxing in his chair while singing to Frank Sinatra, dumbbell presses and curls), and then a record of the day's writing, how many words he'd gotten that day; some days there were only 50, others as many as 1200. And after each and every entry, he'd written: "Thank you."

When he began writing seriously at age eighteen, my father's goal was to write and publish ten books in his lifetime. Including his volume, *Selected Stories*, he published eleven, all of which will endure—I have no doubts about that. And when I want to feel his soul and the souls of the people he wrote about and, ultimately, more of *my* soul, I simply take one his collections off my shelf and begin reading the art he created. But what does not endure is the body that holds all this, and I miss his loud laugh, the wise but mischievous glint in his eye, his hand on my back as I bend forward to hug and kiss him, the soft bristle of his beard against my cheek, the lingering scent of shampoo in his thinning hair; I miss sitting with him on his deck smoking a cigar and drinking a beer or glass of bourbon, talking about writing or teaching or my kids or any of the rest of this rich life; I miss picking up the phone just to tell him a joke I'd heard that day; I miss going to his house with six or seven buddies to play poker or watch a boxing match; I miss watching him flirt with women, seeing the way he captured their imagination, so many over the years in what I believe was, for the most part, a sincere effort to love well; and more than all this, I miss how much bigger life felt when he was still here with us, as if life were a symphony with a full orchestra playing all at once. But now the string section seems to be gone, and the brass too, and God won't make another one like him. The hole he leaves behind is big and dark and quiet. So quiet.

But it's the kind of quiet he would feel called to fill with words, true words that form sentences that become paragraphs that turn into pages that, with faith and perseverance, yield stories. So let's tell some here in this volume about the old man and his work and his life. I was blessed to see almost forty years of it, which began for me with my father and mother still in their twenties in Iowa City, Pop sitting us down each night to tell us stories of Running Blue Ice Water and his family, Dad's eyes shiny and alert, his cheeks flushed, his arms and hands moving, his voice full of the joy that comes with making something, his accent still southern Louisiana, this young man who would one day become one of the truly great short story writers of America, my father, Andre Dubus.

Andre Dubus

"SWM"

—from a letter to a friend on July 8, 1988:

"Pills aren't working (adrenaline from the workshop, from the work I'm trying to do on the long essay, and this hiatus of joy— probably ephemeral, but ain't they all?), so I lay in bed amusing myself, and came up with this—

"SWM, 52, good physical condition except for amputated left leg and crippled right one; largely confined to wheelchair; fiction writer, divorced father of six who despises money and is presently living on credit, seeks companionship of female with or without children, who loves the sea, beaches, woods, sky, weather, drinking in bars, jazz and country and opera, lying idly in the sun, reading fiction and poetry, a spurner of psychobabble and psychotherapy, who strives for a spiritual life while remaining hedonistic; must be witty and kind, good to my six-year-old and eighteen-month-old daughters, resilient and passionate; must not love money and things but must enjoy smoking and other such pleasures of the flesh, like daylight and nocturnal lovemaking, and pleasurable distractions, like movies and idle talk, and must have a car till I can buy one. Honesty absolutely required, and spontaneous, justified and even loud and obscene anger are not essential, but would season the relationship. This is not all fun in the sun but a durable, graceful dance to the music of mortality. Former nuns of light heart are welcome."

Tributes

left the refrigerator stopped him. On his
first ~~morning at~~ morning at home he tried
to turn between the counter and
refrigerator by lowering his legrests; when
he pressed the switch to release them, they
dropped quickly, and he gasped at the
blades of pain in his feeling legs. Lydia bent
down and grabbed his ankles and lifted
them while he moaned and began to sweat.

3 or
        His feet in their casts would not
fit under the long rectangular mahogany
~~table~~ table in the dining room, so he
sat parallel to his end of it, removed
the right arm rest of the wheelchair and
ate, as he said, side-saddle. He looked
to his right at his food and Lydia.

"The Colonel's Wife"
2nd draft

Andre Dubus

Lee K. Abbott

My Dinner with Andre. Not.

It is 1979, and I am in my second year as an assistant professor of English at Case Western Reserve University in Cleveland. I have, I believe, only seven or eight published stories at this time, all of them impossibly clever and shallow—the evidence, if you will, a smarty-pants leaves behind when he is largely indifferent to the words he's leaving between margins—but I nonetheless imagine myself on the verge of making literary history, a fellow but for a lucky break or two about to twist time in the direction of beauty. (And, of course, bucks.) My creative writing colleague in those days was the late Robert Wallace, a poet perhaps more well known, sadly so, for his textbook, *How to Write Poetry*, than for any of his several hundred artful instances of the "best possible words in the best possible order." It is late spring and Bob has appeared at my office door to present me with a book, Andre's *Separate Flights*, the volume with the unappealingly grainy yellow cover. Did I know this fellow's stories, Bob asked.

No, I had to admit, I did not. It was an admission of deepest ignorance, I understand now, like not knowing, sheesh, who Little Richard was or who walked first on the moon. "Here," Bob said. "Learn something." And, over the next few days, I did. A lot, in fact.

At the time, I was much enamoured of those writers—Barry Hannah, for example, and Harry Crews—who seemed to leave the page scorched in their efforts to account for the to and fro of our condemned and crooked kind. I was a fan, too, of Welty, in particular that Miss Eudora who talked that talk peculiar to folks named, oh, Poppa-Daddy and Uncle Beebum. I was still wrought up with Faulkner, of course, who'd taught me even at thirteen the meaning of words like "lubricious" and "miasma," language a thirteen-year-old boy probably ought not to yet know. I'd done my time with Hemingway, never warming to the spare and close-mouthed sort he was on the page. I still loved F. Scott F., especially at story-length (see, for example, "Winter Dreams" for still another illustration of what the landscape looks like this side of paradise). I'd loved Dorothy Parker for about five minutes, Anthony Burgess for a whole summer. Walker Percy was a current favorite, as was the horror and heartbreak that came from the business end of Hubert Selby's pen. It was, you're right to guess, reading not eclectic, but haphazard—books that could have fallen from the back of a highjacked bookmobile for all the sense it made.

Then came Andre, that writer who seemed to know the why of our what. His was the story of a generous sensibility, a story that meant to account for all that might animate and explain. His were people wonderfully bent—people, as the poet once put it, in love with things about to vanish. His were the moments you found not in the newspaper or on TV, but on your block, in your apartment, at your school. Most of all, for me at least, his were stories, even about matters domestic, done BIG, fiction that meant to take its time getting to the rank and cold and dumb we are. His was fiction as history, authoritative and instructive. His was fiction, I have since learned, that cost him more than time to get on the page right.

Here was art, I may have said to Bob a day or two later, that had spine and gland and gut, a fiction that as much took the measure of you as you of it. Here was a fiction of grace and felicitous form. No sleight of hand here, no hootchy-koo, no aesthetic peekaboo, no fancyschmancy. Just stories, one after the other after the other, fine and meet as angels.

Now to the dinner and the far-too-precious title you shook your head over to get here. It's the middle nineties now, and I have set up shop at The Ohio State University in Columbus (they insist upon the The, honest). By this time, I've published five books, none of them perfect. I am a professor of the Full sort, which means I get paid a lot for the lies I tell, but I am still reading, and learning from, Andre. In fact, I had reviewed his selected stories, that hefty and necessary volume, for the *Chicago Tribune*. I read him through the accident, read him through his silence. I read his essays, those tender, if brief insights into the he and she we vessels are. I read the people who had evidently learned to write in his living room. Peter Orner was an acquaintance, Christopher Tilghman a fellow traveler. I read Andre's son. Unaccountably, however, I had not made contact with him, something I usually do when a story demands a "thank you."

Then I get an invitation to give a reading at now defunct Bradford College in Haverhill, Andre's former employer. My host is to be Perry Glazer, himself a teller of tales. I accept, part of my fantasy the idea that Andre will be at my reading, maybe in the front row, maybe smiling, maybe pounding his hands in joy. Such, really, is almost the first thing out of my mouth when Perry picks me up at Logan: "You think Andre Dubus will be there?" Perry shrugs. He doesn't know. Could be, could be not. "Maybe I could go over to his house," I say. "Tell him howdy or something." Sure, Perry says. He'll give Andre a call.

So I do the reading that evening. No Andre. Scandalously little of the thunderous applause I meant God to hear. Instead of an hour or so of splendid badinage with the man in question, I spend the evening with a former student and her intended who've driven up from Cambridge. I drink too much firewater. I get silly, profoundly so. The next day Perry takes me to a casino in Connecticut, where he wins nearly six hundred dollars playing blackjack and I buy tax-free cigarettes from a tribe happy to give the finger to Uncle Sam. "Andre?" I say on the drive back. Perry had called, I learned, left a message. Maybe this evening, maybe dinner. Andre's choice.

In the hotel room, I pace. Suddenly, and incredibly, meeting Andre Dubus seems like the worst idea since sin. What would I say that he hadn't heard before? How small will the small talk get? Christ, what if he's actually read my work, even the fittest of it, and has decided that it is to the art what the minnow is to Moby? What if, in person, he turns out to be so much less than he is in print? Back to the firewater, I confess. And back again.

Too soon it is nighttime, and Perry is at my door. Andre can't make it, he says. He's not feeling well.

Ah, I say. I nod. I nod a couple more times. Nodding seems like the best thing to do with my head for the five minutes it takes us to get to the restaurant. Then, owing to my eccentric circuitry, I am, well, ticked off. I have been insulted, I conclude. Maligned. At this very minute, I imagine, Andre Dubus, big shot *écrivain*, is rolled up in front of his TV, having more than a laugh or two at my vanity. While I'm hacking away at a steak, Andre Dubus is on the phone to a true pal, the pair of them saddened by my presumptuousness. That LKA should presume to break bread with—well, you get the idea.

And, sometime before the dessert is set afire, so do I. The man is sick, I tell myself. Grow the dickens up.

Then I am home, and time is passing, too much of it uneventfully, and one day Andre Dubus is dead, the only news in the newspaper that day, and I find I've still not written him to say thanks. So here it is then—for him in the outer darkness from me in the inner: thanks for your imagined real world, for the purl and sweep of the sentence; thanks for your passion for the least of us; thanks for your strangers, the many he's and she's you typed to life; thanks for the nails and lumber and paint and screws you made us believe in; thanks for the wishes and the dreams, however evanescent and crosswise; thanks for the telling and the glorious showing.

Thank you, Andre Dubus, for the flesh made word.

Lee K. Abbott's most recent collection of stories is *Wet Places at Noon.*

Marilyn Abildskov

Eggs

Two years after *Broken Vessels* came out, a friend sent me the paperback edition. She knew I was a fan of Andre Dubus and his fiction. She knew, too, that I craved the written word in a way I hadn't before and haven't since. I was living in a small city in the center of Japan at the time, teaching English to junior high school students, studying karate, and falling in love. With black-haired students. With light through my *shoji* doors. With smell of bonfires during *obon*. And, eventually, with one particular man.

The man was 37-years-old and had never married, and I was 32 and very much compelled and neither one of us was fluent in the other's language, but we managed for some time to communicate happily and abundantly the way two people genuinely interested in one another do. We kept dictionaries between us and opened their tissue-thin pages frequently, which gave our conversations a slow, ritualized quality, as if each word were scripture. I had been living in this small city for several years by then but remained woefully tongue-tied when it came to Japanese. Too many words sounded distressingly close. Bridge and chopsticks, fireworks and cherry blossoms—I couldn't hear the difference between these pairs in Japanese. Sometimes, when I stopped in at a certain jazz cafe, the elegant proprietor who wore white shirts buttoned to the neck would ask if the notes I scribbled onto white legal pads were part of a novel, and I would try to answer in my haphazard borrowed tongue, *no not a novel, just a letter*, only I would confuse the word *letter* for *egg*, saying, *no not a novel, I'm just writing an egg*.

Things didn't work out between this 37-year-old man and me and, in time, our conversations turned cold and spare so that each time we spoke, it felt as if we were sitting uncomfortably in a room with no furniture or cushions or anything at all. One night I told him that I didn't know where I stood with him, that he seemed to withdraw a little more every day, and he had said that if that's how I saw him, as distant or cold, then my perspective was as good as true, and though I wanted to argue, to say that I didn't think he was cold, that that was just something I said to find out what he thought, I didn't because words that night had come to seem dangerous, something I couldn't trust to accomplish anything more than getting us more tangled up and confused.

When you believe you no longer love, you no longer do. So wrote Andre Dubus in "On Charon's Wharf," one of the essays I remember reading from *Broken Vessels* round about the same time I was falling in love and then out of sorts with a certain foreign country and foreign man. I remember with a clarity that surprises me still how certain phrases muscled their way in. *So many of us fail: we divorce wives and husbands, we leave the roofs of our lovers, go once again into the lonely march. . . . With words we create genies . . . words are complex: at times too powerful or fragile or simply wrong; and they are affected by a tone of voice, a gesture of a hand, a light in the eyes . . . what I want and want to give, more than the intimacy of words, is shared ritual, the sacraments.*

The spine on that book remains broken on pages 78 and 79, a physical reminder that I returned again and again to a certain passage in which Dubus writes that, despite failures, he still believes in love's possibility, in its presence on the earth, in the potential to approach the altar on any morning of any day which may be the last and receive the touch that does not say there is no death but instead says,

> In this instant I recognize, with you, that you must die. And I believe I can do this in an ordinary kitchen with an ordinary woman and five eggs. I scramble them in a saucepan, as my now-dead friend taught me; they stand deeper and cook softer he said. I take our plates, spoon eggs on them, we sit and eat. She and I and the kitchen have become extraordinary: we are not simply eating; we are pausing in the march to perform an act together; we are in love and the meal offered and received is a sacrament which says: I know you will die; I am sharing food with you; it is all I can do, and it is everything.

It is everything, this ability certain writers have to endow ordinary people and ordinary events with extraordinary wisdom and extraordinary light. Dubus did as much again and again as he wrote about running and railroads and love between living creatures and the sky and the sea, reminding us with each essay that the word can be made flesh, that the flesh, though imperfect, is all we've got. *We are of the flesh, and we must turn with faith toward that truth.* I see him as an old-fashioned essayist, someone unafraid to leave the crook of narrative to say what he thinks but someone whose candor never forgets its basic modesty. In Dubus, modesty is no gimmick, no mask for persona on the page, as it so often is for other practitioners of the form; instead his modesty is an integral part of an attempt to articulate a deeply moral vision of the universe, one that affirms the mysteries of love and longing in all of their complexities.

In "Messages," from *Meditations from a Movable Chair,* he describes an incident late on a certain Sunday morning when, as he sat in his wheelchair on the sun deck taking in grass, blue skies, birds, and trees, he heard the phone ring and then, after four rings, the machine pick up.

> I had Sinatra on the tape: he sang a line, then I spoke, then Sinatra sang another line. The caller listened to this for ten or twelve seconds, then talked. I did not know him; he sounded like a workingman, and in his voice were nuances of longing and affection. He said: "Betsy? This is Dave." I turned my wheelchair around and went through the door. "I haven't seen you in a while." I pushed down the hall. "If you'd like to get together, maybe we could meet tonight at that place we like." I turned into the dining room, wheeled toward the kitchen, to the telephone on the wall. "Okay, I hope to see you there." As I passed the telephone, I grabbed it, listened to a dial tone, wished he had left a number.

In the first paragraph of the essay, then, Dubus establishes action: this is a piece about a message left mistakenly on his answering machine. And he begins to openly imagine a life for the voice on the machine: that the man sounds like a workingman; that in this man's voice are nuances of longing and affection. As Dubus continues, he becomes more contemplative; he begins to fill in the gaps. His imagination, in other words, becomes the story itself.

> So she knew his number, or he did not want to be called. It could be adultery or other cheating. But she was not the

unfaithful one; he would have hung up when Betsy did not answer. Maybe he was married, or living with a woman, and Betsy shared a place with a man who was neither her husband nor love, so Dave heard my voice and still spoke to the machine. Maybe erotic love was not an element. But something had been in his voice, and he had not named the place where he wanted to be with her.

There is heat in the way Dubus describes what the man has called "that place we like" as an unnamed place. And this absence of names stands in contrast to the way Dubus begins his essay by offering names, by giving *them* names, these two people whose names he does not know, cannot know, these two people whose voices he reads, which is to say imagines his way into. *I am giving them different names*, he begins, so that by the essay's end, there is a sense that Dubus is doing more than simply getting himself off the hook, being "truthful" in an airtight, journalistic way. *I am giving them different names*, he says, and by doing so—by using a utilitarian admission to full and artful effect—Dubus creates them, these people, in compassion rather than judgment, and saturates the essay in that complicated truth that wisdom truly is, rather than reducing them to categories as simplistic accuracy might demand, showing the reader that this situation to which Dubus has had only a glimpse is about something that requires new names, that the words "adultery" or "cheating" are not enough for this unnamed place in longing and affection that we, too, now like.

The Japanese man and I got tangled up in our words that night that I called him cold when I didn't think he was, and when he told me he considered me *toku betsu ni*, meaning *special* or *important*, I heard only the *betsu ni*, meaning *to separate*. We did, in fact, separate just a few days later when I boarded a plane bound for the United States and spent the next seven years trying to write a book about him that I thought of as a love letter to him or maybe a small and delicate egg, but before that, before our separate lives began, we shared one last meal, which we didn't know would be our last.

We stood in his small kitchen. He cut the tomatoes while I watched the pasta cook. I had gone to a great deal of trouble to track down a jar of artichoke hearts for our meal and had hoped he would like them, this delicacy he'd never tried, but after one bite, he grimaced and said they were too sour and I picked them out of the pasta and ate the hearts alone that night.

When I think back on that meal now I think of the odd tenderness that passed between two people who had once been very much in love, and how extraordinary that was, making dinner in his small kitchen and eating at his low table and speaking so easily. And I think too of what passes between reader and writer, that secret attachment that forms in the middle of the night, the way one man's words muscle their way into another woman's skin. There's no good word, I suppose, for the various attachments of our lives, least of all those between lovers who part company and never see each other again or readers and writers who never meet except through the sacrament of words on the page. Only the solace of memory remains: a meal of pasta and artichoke hearts; a paperback book with a broken spine; muscular prose about men and women and fallibility and grace; and a passage I return to again and again regarding communion and five scrambled eggs.

Marilyn Abildskov's essays and stories have appeared in *Black Warrior Review, Sonora Review, Puerto del Sol, Fourth Genre*, and *Quarterly West*.

Donald Anderson

Into the Silence

In 1962, I intended to quit high school to work full-time in a car wash. My best friend had dropped out to work there and, in what seemed a short time, purchased a 1947 Pontiac sport coupe. I informed my father of my plans. He informed me of his. Two years after, public high school diploma in hand, I started college. My announced major was engineering—the degree my father would have sought had he had the reasonable fortune to skip an alcoholic father, the Depression, rheumatic fever, sleeping sickness, copper mines, a blinded eye, and an early family.

What I remember from first-year calculus is my professor, Mr. Smith— "Call me, 'Mister,' not 'Professor.'" Then: "Doctors repair worlds. They don't dismantle." He'd worked on the periphery of the Manhattan Project—knew Edward Teller, he said, Oppenheimer, Enrico Fermi. Adam Smith was a drunk. One day he arrived late for class. He selected a chalk and began a white line, waist-high across the board. When he came to the end of the board, he continued. In fact, he drew a line across the windows and around the room. At the doorway, by which he'd entered, he turned. "Even that's not infinity," he said. He cast us a lenient but morose look, then left. After one year of college, I, too, departed. For France. I stayed three years. I did learn French, but when I returned home and to school, my new major was English.

In time, I became an English professor, until, dissatisfied in my forties, I stopped to go back to school. I'd wearied of students' (and faculty's) Cliffs Note versions of Beowulf, Ahab, Lear, the Brothers K, Nick Carraway, and Daisy Miller. I didn't believe I could face another essay with the phrase "Heart of Darkness" or *Sturm und Drang* in its footnotes or title, surrounded by harried prose. Then I heard myself in a department meeting: "Look. The principal feature of Shakespeare's work is hardly that he was a middle-class, middle-aged, white European male.

Get a grip! Christ." I applied to and—luck of luck—was admitted to the M.F.A. program at Cornell University. There, with bright and able children—most of them half my age—I wrote stories. I suppose I'd always wanted to. By this time, I'd negotiated divorce and a second marriage, complete with children and step-children, pets and step-pets, aging parents, and my own near death on an emergency surgical table. I admit I felt I had stories to tell.

It was during this period in my life that I discovered Andre Dubus, his essays and stories, many of which were being published in EPOCH, Cornell's literary magazine. I responded immediately. Maybe it was because my own life and reading had caught up to the human and fictional territory Andre had for so long staked out and mined. The day later came when Andre called to place work. As the journal's editor I accepted his story—one from what would be his last collection, *Dancing After Hours*—but with an apology about the payment we could afford. I knew of an essay he had written in which he informed he preferred to publish in literary quarterlies and journals rather than in "slicks." In this essay he recounts being published in *The New Yorker* and *Penthouse*, wherein he uncomfortably found his work amid "advertisements for things that exclude all but the rich," and in the case of *Penthouse*, "among the crotches." His essay refers to publishing in *Sewanee Review*. This story on which he'd worked 17 months, through 7 drafts and 400 pages (resulting in 60), earned him 500 bucks. But the story, he wrote in his essay, no matter its worth, had been given a dignity he could see: "On those pages it lives alone, untouched by paper genitals, diamonds and gold."

When Andre called in the 1990s to place work, I believed he believed what he'd written in his essay some twenty years before, but I also knew that since that time, he'd been maimed by a passing car that had torn off one leg and ruined the other when he'd stopped at night to assist some people in a stalled car. I knew, too, he'd suffered long hospital stays, a divorce, and the loss of the custody of children, and long periods during which he could neither write nor work as a teacher. I apologized again for the small sum my journal could offer. With no hint of a pitied self, he said, "That's two weeks groceries."

After his story was published, we wrote a few times and talked on the phone. On the day before I read of his death, I'd by chance re-read his essay "Into the Silence," which ends:

Short story writers simply do what human beings have always done. They write stories because they have to; because they cannot rest until they have tried as hard as they can to write the stories. They cannot rest because they are human, and all of us need to speak into the silence of mortality, to interrupt and ever so briefly stop that quiet flow, and with stories try to understand at least some of it.

A few years back, Andre wrote to me about a story of mine he'd chanced upon. To my great pleasure, he made a point to praise its economy. "I so much admire distillation," he said, writing in pencil on paper torn from a Big Chief tablet, the kind of tablet he would have known we'd both remember from school. True or not, I see Andre writing his stories in longhand—first in pencil on paper—the least technological connection from his hand to his heart to the page. I see him thus armed and scribbling the large and small trespasses we all commit in the name of hope and love and fear and despair and longing.

At the moment, I'm thinking of Andre's "Bastille Day," a one-page essay meditating on loss. The essay is actually less than a page, though it escorts us through a family album beginning with French ancestors storming the tower mid-summer in the 1780s to Louisiana and a father's death in the 1960s on to a mother's death in the 1980s, and so on implicitly to what is now Andre's very own departure. Meantime in a ferociously distilled work, we, with Andre, endure the loss of three wives and what he dubs the "daily and nightly living with six children," the loss of one leg and the use of the other in a random and terrible wreck, and the confinement of a vital ex-Marine to a mechanical chair.

It has taken me more than one page to maneuver about the loss I feel in Andre Dubus' absence. He has, however, in his fiction and essays, left us *this*: it is not the work of art to make order, but to complicate order in just such a way that it begins to resemble living.

Donald Anderson's collection *Fire Road* won Iowa's 2001 John Simmons Short Fiction Award.

Doris Betts

Human and Holy Loving

I met Andre Dubus only once, at the Wesleyan University Writers Conference. That summer in Connecticut he was a vigorous and attractive man with an ex-marine's swagger, who collected at all times such a cluster of female admirers that the clump of women would be noticed first, drifting as a unit from building to building like a bee swarm and he at its center.

I had not then read his novel *The Lieutenant,* published when he was 30, but already admired his story collections, and, watching the bevy flutter here and there about the campus, I thought that his obvious enjoyment of women's company might underlie his growing skill in writing their stories in their voices.

Yet, as all nine of his books were eventually to show, the women living in both his life and on his pages were not always admirers, even lovers. He said in his last interview, "I don't think, it's experimental to write from the point of view of a woman. I think, it's just imagining."

That imagination had range, as just a few female characters from his stories will call to mind: the woman persuading a teenage boy to murder her husband; those long conversations between LuAnn Arcencaux and Marsha; Polly in "The Pretty Girl"; Edith's affair with an ex-priest; Catherine, who learns her husband is having an affair, or, in a different story, Jackie the college girl who has realized that even her father is an adulterer; Rusty after a shark attack; bartender Emily; the mother Claire giving monologues to daughter Molly over cocktails; Anna Griffin; Leslie in California where Kevin has blackened her eye, an old woman whose husband dies in the night in their shared bed.

Joyce Carol Oates has said that Dubus had "deep commitment" to his characters. He described his process as "becoming one," for example, "with the woman and the evil she chose in 'The Last Moon.'"

But besides his vividly imagined women, there were real women in his life as well—three of them divorced wives (Patricia, 12 years, four children; Tommie Gail, two years; Peggy Rambach, 10 years, two children). Ex-wives get some mention in his essays, though with reticence. He seems to take his own and his fictional failed marriages as just more evidence of quotidian fallibility, and both author and husband avoid the occasion for blame.

Instead, he gives more space in the nonfiction to his sister Kathryn's rape, an account of his teaching Hemingway to high school girls; how wife Pat did not stay overnight in the Plaza Hotel; the nameless woman he courted by telephone; the first altar girl he saw at Sunday mass; a meeting with actress Liv Ullmann; and the unlikely coincidence of encountering a woman who actually witnessed the highway accident that at age 49 put Dubus in a wheelchair for life.

And above all these other females are his daughters, especially the younger two. Cadence and Madeleine, the latter still in the womb when the speeding car struck him. The girls are most fully rendered in his title essay in *Broken Vessels* (1991). Primary custody of both daughters went to his third wife after their obviously painful divorce.

By his own literary content Dubus himself made it impossible for us to give him a reading unaffected by the pre- and post-reality of that accident which cleaved across his life deep as the Grand Canyon across Arizona. When I first heard that he had been hit on Route 93 between Boston and Haverhill, July 23, 1986, where he had stopped to help a woman stalled by the highway, then heard that he had lost his left leg and might not even live, there leapt to mind the memory of that virile young man with his cohort of summer-girl writers; and I wondered then if the parable of the Good Samaritan had been revised to put an injured damsel-in-distress by the roadside, might even the Priest and the Levite have stopped?

Dubus' essay "Lights of the Long Night" vividly retells how he stopped, how the other car did not, and all the pain and despair that followed.

Another writer, my friend Reynolds Price, was also mowed down and now lives in a wheelchair, though what felled him was not a speeding car but a secret cancer that had been coiling itself snakelike about his spine for years. Neither man sought nor has even tolerated cloying sentimentality about their stoicism, about finding their creativity deepened by hardship, and their character honed and uplifted, etc., etc., etc. But both men have written bluntly about their pain, depressions, their long mental and physical struggles—Price in *A Whole New Life*, and Dubus in *Broken Vessels* and *Meditations from a Movable Chair*. If I were here to mouth on their behalf easy platitudes about the value of suffering, no doubt an army of disabled brethren and sistern would justifiably run me down with wheelchairs and beat me to death with crutches.

Yet it is true that both authors have written their most profound prose after a hard descent into such unexpected, undeserved suffering, and that in those depths both experienced a ripening of religious experience—Price through his rather private, even mystic, Protestantism, Dubus by way of ongoing Catholic worship that included home prayers as well as the daily Eucharist whenever possible.

Wrote Patrick Samway, S.J., in *Image* magazine: Dubus' last 25 essays reveal his "constant post-biped struggle to appreciate God's infinite love for him." He risked in "A Woman in April" making clear that some human bodies may seem outwardly sound and yet contain crippled hearts. Like Price, Dubus became increasingly open about his Catholicism and its necessity for his survival, so much so that even readers who had not previously read Dubus' work were arrested by a quotation in a *NYTBR* article after his death February 24, 1999. It came from his essay explaining why an almost obsessively macho man finally gave up his longtime ownership of handguns, though after Dubus became an invalid he also presumably was at greater risk of being a helpless victim of burglary or assault. "I gave up answers that are made of steel that fire lead," wrote Dubus, "and decided to sit in a wheelchair on the frighteningly invisible palm of God."

If accident and circumstance taught him that approach to immobility and dependence, they also only deepened ideas that seem foreshadowed in his earlier work. One of my favorites, "A Father's Story," appeared before his accident in a 1983 collection, *The Times Are Never So Bad*. Three fathers operate in the story: horseman Luke Ripley, who deeply loves his daughter Jennifer; the Catholic Father Paul LeBoeuf, a friend who regularly hears Luke's confession; and God the Father, to whom in the end Luke is praying through Christ. After Jennifer, who has probably drunk too much beer, drives her car into and kills a pedestrian, Luke takes on the whole weight of that event. He finds the dying victim and leaves him there to be discovered by others, deliberately drives her damaged car into a tree in St. John's churchyard, and asks to receive the Eucharist but not to make confession first. In fact he never confesses to anyone human what he has done, but tells God "I would do it again." The story ends with the back-and-forth of his prayer-dialectic with Jesus who "never had a daughter," while Luke loves his more than he loves truth. "Then you love in weakness," come the words from Heaven, followed by Luke's reply: "As you love me."

This equating of human with divine love and parenthood has its later counterpart in the autobiographical essay "Broken Vessels," in a collection published five years after his injury and amputation. Now as his marriage ends, Dubus is losing his two young daughters and he—like the fictional Luke Ripley—cries out in prayer to Christ: "So You had three years of public life which probably weren't so bad, were probably even good most of the time, and You suffered for three days, from Gethsemane to Calvary, but You never had children taken away from you."

Time and pain have expanded Dubus' fatherly love for his children to a magnitude as great, and as difficult, as that of Luke Ripley for his daughter.

"A Woman in April" seems in line with my memory of Dubus at Wesleyan, as the wheelchair-bound author enjoys the sight of New York's beautiful women, even complimenting one close by and getting back spontaneous warmth and a smile. Her quick and natural reaction has illustrated to him that most people feel love and compassion, though often we "cannot or will not see these barely visible wounds of other human beings," people not so easily identified as crippled. So we fail to telephone or visit or write a note or "make some other seemingly trifling gesture to give to someone what only we, and God, can give: an hour's respite, or a day's, or a night's; and sometimes more than respite, sometimes joy."

The beautiful woman who paused to smile has given him joy, though he does not expect her to change immediately into Mother Teresa or Dorothy Day. "No," he ends the essay, "she is one of us, and what she said and did on that April evening was, like the warm sunlit sky, enough: for me, for the end of winter, for the infinite possibilities of the human heart."

That image of the unknown, smiling, beautiful woman who has turned and responded to the older Dubus makes a stronger image that superimposes itself atop my Wesleyan memory, and finally blurs all those girls who once swirled in a Maypole dance around him. Obviously I had, at that time, no real knowledge at all of who Andre Dubus was. And for all his early talent, he could have known very little of the writer and the man he would become.

Doris Betts' story collection *Beasts of the Southern Wild and Other Stories* has been reissued by Scribner.

James Lee Burke

Baseball and Race

When my first cousin Andre Dubus and I were boys in south Louisiana, we devoted most of our summer days, in one way or another, to playing or watching baseball. It was in the era before television, when major league games came to us only on radio and bush league ball was a vital part of southern life. You knew the players around town; they ran filling stations or worked as carpenters or meat-cutters. But on a twilight diamond, right after a rain, with halos of mist glowing around the electric lamps high overhead, these same blue-collar men had all the mythic and carnival characteristics of national celebrities. There was also a reckless physical courage about them, an outrageous disdain for convention that we intuitively recognized as the elements that made them a separate race, a collection of boy-men who would never grow up, who would always be out of sync with the world, always spitting Brown Mule on the shoes of authority.

They threw spitters and beanballs, came in with their spikes up, and busted up double plays with elbows and knees. Sometimes the batter deliberately slung the bat at the pitcher's head like a helicopter blade. They smoked in the dugout and, in view of the crowd, rubbed their bats between their thighs like they were masturbating. Their profanity and yelled insults could leave an uninitiated listener stunned and disbelieving.

Like the men I would work with later in the oil field and on the pipeline, most of their insults had do with oral sex or sodomy, since the implications were what they feared most in themselves. "Cocksucker" was a word they never seemed able to wear out.

Early every morning we gathered at a dirt lot off St. Mary Boulevard in Lafayette and chose up sides. We tried to imitate professional ballplayers in every way we could. We rolled the brims of our hats into virtual cones, and folded, creased, and taped down the crowns at night so they were always sharply peaked in front. We shot the bone and talked as obscenely as we dared, spit through our teeth, straddled our legs, and pridefully hitched up our genitalia.

But we were ahead of our Evangeline League heroes in one respect. Even though Jackie Robinson and Larry Doby had integrated the majors, the minor leagues in the South were still all-white. Some mornings at our dirt-lot games, the children of black lawn men in the neighborhood wandered over and joined us. Few of them had caps, which cost one dollar at Bell's Sporting Goods, and none of them ever had a glove.

Andre had caddied for his father at the city golf course and had cut lawns all summer to buy a claw mitt. It had cost sixteen dollars, in a time when even white adults were paid only three dollars and fifty cents for a ten-hour day of physical labor. Andre rubbed the new leather with oil until it was the color of mahogany, and at night he cupped a ball deep in the pocket and crisscrossed and tied down the glove's sides with twine to give it shape and depth.

It was the kind of glove that you carry all the way through your adolescence, that hangs from your handlebars, that sits on your bookshelf at night like a sentinel, that you entrust to your girlfriend as an act of faith while you're at bat, until the dream becomes just that and you give it up and ballparks become places where you buy a ticket to watch someone else play.

A tall black kid, maybe sixteen years old, who wore jeans with no knees and tennis shoes that were bursting at the toes, showed up at the lot one morning with four other black kids and asked to play. He was already hot and dirty from lawn work and he kept pulling at his T-shirt with his pinched fingers to shake the blades of grass off his stomach and back.

His first time at bat he nailed our best pitcher's hanging curve all the way to the street. It looked like a BB disappearing into the trees. But it was when we watched him play at first base that we knew he was better than any of us. In the first inning he played without a glove and didn't ask for the loan of one; in the second inning Andre lent him his claw mitt. With a runner on first, the black kid vacuumed a line drive out of the dirt, rifled the ball to the second baseman for the automatic out, then caught a wild return throw and flicked his tennis shoe behind him and touched the bag before the batter could make first base.

At the end of the game the black kids were getting on their bikes to rejoin their fathers, the lawn men. I saw Andre hitting his fist into the pocket of his glove. He kept doing it almost as though he were mad at it. Then, as though a troubling thought had finally done its injury and gone its way, he walked over to the black first baseman and tapped him on the arm with the glove.

"You keep it," he said.

"Keep what?"

"You play a lot better with it than I do. You keep the claw."

"What you talkin' about, man?"

"I want you to have it. I told you," Andre said.

We were all silent.

"You foolin' wit' me?" the black kid said.

Andre shook his head. The black kid looked at his friends, then extended his left hand and wrapped his fingers around the soft folds of leather.

"You sure now? 'Cause if you foolin' wit' me—" He made a fist with his right hand and lifted it in the air, but he was smiling when he did it.

I never asked Andre why he gave his glove away because I already knew, and the explanation was not the one he had offered the black kid, nor even the one, in my opinion, that he later offered himself. He gave it away because he didn't believe the white race deserved what it had. Our superior standard of living was at best a gift, just as an artist's talent is a gift, but we had become prideful and racially arrogant and deliberately obtuse and had murdered the gift of charity in our hearts by denying the simple biological fact of our brotherhood.

The end of this brief story actually took place ten years later, in the barber shop across from the old Lafayette city police station and jailhouse. The station and jail were three stories tall and built of gray stone, and on the narrow apron of lawn in front was a Confederate monument, the color of burnished lead, that looked like it had been placed there as an afterthought. Back in the 1950s the electric chair used to travel from parish to parish; when it came to Lafayette the two big power generators were parked on a semi under the trees on a side street, and workmen in coveralls would string the long, rubber-coated cables to the third floor of the jail where the condemned man was electrocuted at midnight.

It had started to rain, and one of the barbers had opened the front door to let in the cool air. I could see a black man at a barred window on the third floor of the jail, his forearms propped across the windowsill.

I had just gotten my first paycheck as an English instructor at the university, and I decided to have a shoeshine.

The porter, who wore a starched gray apron, a whisk broom in his back pocket, and who was about my age, bent to his work and popped his rags across my shoes. But each time he straightened up to get more polish or reach for a brush, his eyes lingered for a moment on my face. Then I remembered.

"Did you used to play ball over on St. Mary Boulevard?" I asked.

"Yes, sir, I did."

"You played first base."

"That's right. You got a good memory. I seen you 'round town, but I didn't think you'd recall me."

"You remember that day about the glove?"

"I ain't forgot it. That's me. It sure is."

"You were a great player, podna."

He nodded and smiled politely, then began buffing the points of my shoes.

Then I asked the question that I shouldn't have asked: "Did you play in high school, or in—"

He stood erect and looked obliquely out the front door. He flipped the shine rag idly in one hand.

"I got married, had to settle down, stop all that runnin' round, you understand what I mean?" he said.

"Yeah, sure."

"You cain't make no money playin' games."

"Yeah, I guess that's right."

"I think about it sometimes, though."

He bent back into his work, then a moment later he tapped the bottom of one shoe with his long fingers to show me that the shine was over.

"See you around," I said when I paid him.

"Yes, sir. I'll be here."

James Lee Burke's story collection, *The Convict and Other Stories*, has been reissued.

Frederick Busch

Andre and the Daughters

I've always thought of Andre as a religious writer. I believe that he actively worshipped his Lord as Roman Catholics require of themselves that they do, and I know that even his toughest, most seemingly earthbound work had to do with the relationship, as he understood it, between humanity and (as he understood it) heaven. Andre carried his God within him, and, for more secular urgencies, a shotgun and an axe handle in the trunk of his car.

He wrote about crusty Marines and beat-up, down-trodden children, and girls whose womanhood did not beckon with promise; and he wrote of men and women whose lives were so far past the promise they once had wished to see that they were, although not old, already looking back. And he wrote these stories of difficult lives with a prose so graceful, so intent on achieving the beauty he believed, he swore, he wished, and maybe even knew was within them, that their dark lives flickered, a little, with the light of his sure, unsentimental language.

He came to Colgate University in the '80s, with Peggy and their infant child—she was breastfed in the back of the room while Andre answered questions up front—and later they napped, all three of them, in our living room. Their ribs rose and fell, it seemed, in unison in the autumn sun that gathered in the house. It was a portrait of plenty, of ease, a fine moment of fullness. And that night Andre read, for what he said was the first time, "A Father's Story." We were in a large room at Colgate, and it was packed. He was pleased but also apprehensive, I thought; so I knew the story mattered to him, for, while he always treated his work and his audience with respect, he was almost worried that night. I believe he suspected that the story was large: that he had woven a seine very well, and he had caught a great creature.

The story is, of course, large and living. It walks the dangerous edge of emotion—his work dares to go there, risking (as we should) sentimentality in order to explore feeling. And it looks directly at, talks directly to, Andre's God and his profound sense of the immensity involved in fathering. It is a great story, and we all, that night, knew it.

One after another, once the silence of expelled breath—we had been struck a blow: he worked physically as well as metaphysically—followed his ending, and once we had taken a breath, I heard sobbing. It came not from one of the more than a hundred people in the room; it came from many. Singly and in clusters, the college women in the audience came forward to tell him of their love for their own father.

"My father would have done that," a student told him between sobs, referring to the fictive father's willingness to break the law to save his daughter, risking cosmic as well as earthly punishment to emulate his Lord.

"Of course he would have, darlin," Andre said, "and you should go out there—I saw a pay phone out there in the hall—and you call him up and tell him you love him."

One by one—I followed to see—they called, as their turn came, and they told their father of the story they'd been read. And then they passed along the message of love they had found in the story.

I do not think he meant to be telling his readers how to live. And he would have bridled at my use of "message," as—even while saying it—I do, too. Andre Dubus did not write scripture lessons or any other kind of lessons. He wrote about the soul in its agonies and occasional triumphs, and he pushed the language—with respect—as hard as he could. He tried to make beauty. And he succeeded. And now he is in our stories. Because of him, they're good ones. But, because he died from us, they all—in spite of the abiding art he left us—end unhappily.

Frederick Busch's most recent collection of stories is *Don't Tell Anyone*.

Alan Cheuse

It's a Sweetheart

Andre Dubus was one of those rare birds, a writer's writer, not hugely well known to the American reading public but lauded by his peers. Writers as unalike as Anne Tyler and Elmore Leonard recognized the burly bearded Louisiana born ex-Marine as a master of short fiction. Story writer Tobias Wolff describes his work as pure and humane, with every sentence just right and yet without any sense of his having labored over any of it. Story writer and novelist Richard Bausch in a *New York Times* review of Dubus' story collection *Dancing After Hours* praised his characters. "We end up cheering for them," Bausch wrote, "because they are courageous or simply plain stubborn, but most of all because they refuse to despair." People who knew him cheered for Dubus himself, a man who had a great deal that he might have despaired about. Despite constant praise by fellow writers and major reviewers, his career never truly soared even as his work mellowed and sharpened, and on a dark night in 1986 in his forty-ninth year, while stopping at the side of a busy highway to assist a motorist in distress, Dubus was hit by a car and lost a leg—spending the last decade and more in a wheelchair. Writing about his new disability, he displayed honesty and ferocity and directness but not a trace of self-pity. Dubus' recent book was a collection of short essays titled *Meditations from a Movable Chair*. In that volume he offered a brief elegy for his friend and fellow fiction writer Richard Yates, a man with his own painful disabilities. "You never complained to me," Dubus wrote.

> You just kept doing it, morning after morning . . . taking your . . . stand against your flesh and circumstance, writing prose that was a blade, a flame, a cloud, a breath. . . . And about all those words you wrote in all your books on my shelf, I say as you used to about a book or story you loved: They're swell . . . they're really swell; it's a sweetheart of a life's work, it's a sweetheart.

About Dubus' work, most everyone who knows it will say the same.

Alan Cheuse's most recent story collection is *Lost and Old Rivers.*

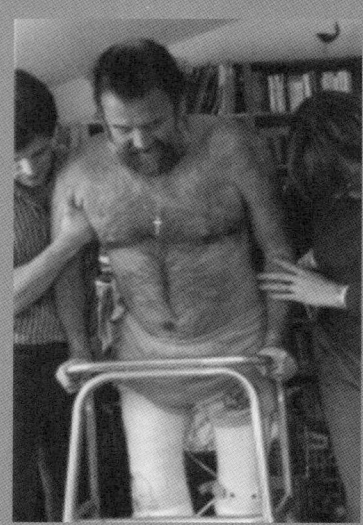

Kathryn Dubus
with Claire Selleck

Brother André

André was always my baby brother. I was six years older than he, with a sister, Beth, in between us. I have so few memories of those growing up years in southern Louisiana but I do remember that André loved to dress up and play soldier and that he had hundreds of those little lead toy soldiers that were so popular in the '40s. As he grew older, baseball became a love and I have memories of him coming home from a neighborhood game, hot and sweaty and happy.

I married in 1951 and started my own home and family. I was living in Lafayette, Louisiana, at that time where André lived with our parents. In January 1954, our parents moved to Lake Charles, Louisiana, and André and I would never live in the same town again.

During the 1950's into the early '60s, there was very little communication between André and me. Perhaps we were both caught up in the self-differentiation throes that often occurs in early adulthood.

My first memories of an adult relationship with André begin in July of 1963 when our father died. We were all gathered around Daddy's bed to tell him goodnight. I knew in my heart that it was goodbye—that Daddy would not live through the night. I remember saying to André, "You'd better tell him that you love him." He replied, "I can't."

There was a terrible rift between my father and my brother. André was a marine at the time—a step he took to please our father. Shortly after Daddy's death, André resigned from the Marines and enrolled in The Writers' Workshop at the University of Iowa. Years later, André told me that Daddy had come to him in a dream and that they had reconciled their differences. I believe this and know that our father would have been proud of the man André became.

The night our father died, André and I were sent to a neighbor's to sleep. We never closed our eyes and talked non-stop until 4:00 a.m. when we were called home. I cannot recall our conversation that night—only that we talked as adults and laid the groundwork for a relationship that would grow stronger through the years.

In the years following our father's death, and after his divorce from his first wife, André would often visit Mother in Lake Charles and I would make the two-hour drive from Baton Rouge to see him. I remember one night going to a bar with André after Mother had gone to bed. We sat there for hours talking and drinking. André said to me, "You are the only woman I know who can drink like a man." Some may not have considered that a compliment, but, coming from my brother, I did.

On another occasion, Mother, André and I went to eat at a restaurant in Lake Charles. The restaurant had a dance area and André and I danced one slow dance. I can still remember the strong sense of maleness and sexuality and enjoyment of the moment that I felt from André. When we returned to our table, Mother commented in a not too complimentary tone, "You two looked like lovers dancing." And we were—lovers of music and rhythm and life.

A Christmas visit to Baton Rouge from André during the late 1970s stands out in my mind. One of our sister's daughters was being presented at a big ball. André was not one for convention and refused to dress up and attend. I agreed to go to New Orleans with him and his wife (André had re-married) in lieu of the ball. I remember a fun day of doing the tourist things and dancing with my brother in the street to the music of a jazz band. We returned to Baton Rouge late and went to our sister's home where a post-ball party was going on. Everyone was dressed very formally and our trio, of course, was very casual—I remember that I wore black and white checked slacks, a black turtleneck sweater and boots. A family friend attending the party said, "Kathryn, you look like a goddamn dyke." This remark infuriated André, and I thought he was going to tear the house apart! His wife and I had to rush him away from the party.

Mother died in 1980. Her death and burial closed doors and memories and experiences. André and I grieved her loss together at her home in Lake Charles. He then returned to Massachusetts while I dealt with the loss of a mother to whom I had become increasingly close.

Then came André's accident in July of 1986. André had stopped to help a young brother and sister whose car had hit an overturned motorcycle on the interstate. As the three of them walked to the median, a car plowed into them, killing the young man instantly. The woman told police that André had pushed her out of the way. André lost his left leg and the use of his right leg and was confined to a wheelchair for the rest of his life. He later told me that as he lay stricken, he saw our Mother, who had died six years earlier, standing just a few feet from him on the highway.

I did not go see André in that first year after the accident. He was in the hospital for a long time and his wife was pregnant with their second child. I think I thought at the time that a visitor was the last thing they needed. But there were phone calls and progress reports. His recovery was slow and painful as he dealt with the loss of his legs and the birth of a child. He experienced deep depression and anger.

In early October of 1987, André called and asked me to come for a visit. He said his wife was overwhelmed by the strain of caring for André and a new baby and was planning to leave him. He wanted me to be a mediator of sorts—a difficult role that I did not look forward to.

The first sight of my brother in a wheelchair brought out all of the old big sister protective instincts. He had been such a physically active man and now seemed so vulnerable. Their home was utter chaos—it was a fairly small home sufficient for two adults and a child. Now there were two children, a wheelchair. I remember books and "stuff" everywhere. I, too, began to feel overwhelmed.

The three of us talked much that weekend, but I knew there was nothing I could do to help. It was apparent to me that the marriage was over and soon after my visit his wife and the girls moved out, leaving André alone.

It was during this 12-year period between 1987 and his death in 1999, that André began to mellow and mature in his relationships. He and I had long phone conversations and grew to know each other more fully and love each other more completely.

There were not many visits during those years. André did not like to fly so travel was difficult for him. He was in Lafayette, Louisiana, for a week in March of 1993 to do a workshop at the University of Southwestern Louisiana. I saw him several times that week and heard him read from one of his own works for the first time. He was famous by then, and I was amazed and proud at the number of people who came to hear him.

In March, 1996, André's new publisher, Alfred A. Knopf, held a reception for him at a bookstore in The Village in New York City. I had a daughter living in New York City at the time and a son flew in from

Albuquerque to meet us. It was such a fun visit—a good family time. Once more, I was impressed by, and proud of, André's talent and fame. I'd always known what a good writer he was, but he was also my baby brother.

Our last visit was in September of 1998. I had a business meeting in New England and flew up a few days early to visit with André and his family. It was a wonderful trip. By this time, André was reconciled with his life and had mended relationships with his children. We had good talks and quality time together. When he drove me to the airport in Boston to meet my travel group, he avoided the interstate where his accident had occurred, saying he still had trouble passing that place on the highway. When I left him, I leaned through the window to kiss him, and he gave me a big smack on the lips and said, "Good-bye Sister Kathryn. I love you." We always called each other Sister Kathryn and Brother André in those later years. That was the last time I saw him.

During the latter part of 1998 and early 1999, there were the phone calls that had become fairly regular. The afternoon of February 24, 1999, there was a message on the answering machine at my office from André. His son, André III, was going to be in Seattle the next day for a reading and signing of his recently published novel, *House of Sand and Fog*. André wanted me to let my son Mark, who lives in Seattle, know.

At 4:50 p.m. CST, I called André. He said he couldn't talk because he had a conference call coming in at 6:00 p.m., his time. The call was to discuss the making of a movie from his short story "The Killing*." I told André that I had received his message and had called Mark and that I would talk to him the next day. He said, "Okay, I love you" and we hung up.

At 10:00 p.m. CST that night, I got a call from my niece, Nicole, that André had died—perhaps just a little over an hour after he and I had talked on the phone. I was overcome with a feeling of total disbelief. I told Nicole several times that this could not be true, since I had talked to André a few hours earlier. Then came an overwhelming sense of grief. I began to shout at Nicole, saying I couldn't talk to her any longer. I hung up and called my youngest daughter. I can remember saying, "My brother is dead and you better come over here." I then called her twin sister and soon both of them were with me. I made calls to my six other children and, somehow, the night passed. The next day, the calls from friends and family began. I was amazed and deeply moved by the outpouring of tributes and recognition for my baby brother, from the front page of *The*

Wall Street Journal to *All Things Considered* on National Public Radio.

At André's funeral, I met so many of the people who had been a part of his life during the years he lived in Massachusetts. I realized how little I really knew about his daily life.

In December of 1991, I was attacked at my back door by a man with a knife. André wrote about my experience in an essay entitled "About Kathryn." He ended the essay with the following paragraph: "This is my sister who wept near the fig tree and grew into a woman who would have killed for her daughter, and who gave God's blessing to the man who came with a knife out of the darkness."

André's words have new meaning for me now. Perhaps André was expressing in that essay the same realization that I had experienced at his funeral—his sense that I had gone from a fifteen-year-old girl weeping near a fig tree to a woman he admired without him really knowing the daily aches and pains, the common struggles and joys that it took for me to get there?

Likewise for me, André had grown from a boy playing with toy soldiers to a man who was a cherished father and friend. From a sweaty nine-year old, he had become an internationally acclaimed writer. But I knew very little about the daily ins and outs of what it took for him to get there.

Sheer physical distance kept André and me from knowing the daily nuances of each other's adult lives and this saddens me at times. But I also remember that dance with my brother so many years ago in Lake Charles and, in a much greater sense, I know that André and I share something that transcends daily human existence—we share a common heart and a common soul. Until we meet again, Brother André.

---

* The movie based on "The Killing" was filmed after André's death and was titled *In The Bedroom*, featuring Sissy Spacek in the lead role. The film was premiered at the Sundance Film Festival in January 2001. Miramax has purchased the distribution rights.

Kathryn Dubus lives in Baton Rouge, Louisiana, as does her daughter, **Claire Selleck**.

David R. Godine

Semper Fidelis

I first encountered the work of Andre Dubus in a modest cafe in New York City while taking the agent Philip Spitzer out to a spartan lunch. I don't believe the cost of the meal exceeded $15.00, but the real treasure that emerged was a manila envelope of Andre's short stories that Phil obviously admired enormously and was totally unable to sell anywhere. I took the stories home, read them, was enormously moved, and called the next morning with some derisory offer. I remember commenting on the writing, and observing that the man behind it must have been a person of strong character—there was an incontrovertible moral core than ran through every story, and one came away with the sense of a personality whose values in life were resolutely formed and relatively unalterable. Phil suggested that I speak to Andre over the phone before we proceeded, and this conversation, which Andre recalled more vividly than I do, was evidently memorable because not once did I try, or even suggest, that he push himself in the direction of a novel. I remember him using a typical baseball analogy: "There are hitters who slam consistent singles and those who punch out an occasional home run. I'm one of the former." That was good enough for me. I recall observing that there was more punch contained in one Dubus short story than in 99.98% of all the novels being published. I still feel that way.

That manila envelope emerged the following year as *Separate Flights*, Andre's first short story collection, and it received glowing reviews everywhere. Other than our enthusiasm for the man and his work, we probably had little to do with this. We were (and remain) a tiny house, and nobody was picking up on the book because it had "Godine" stamped on its spine. It was really the quality of the writing that carried it—and his later books—in the minds of the media, and the hearts of readers.

In all, we published five collections of short stories, one novella, a fat selection of his best stories, and, finally, his first collection of nonfiction, *Broken Vessels*. This last was published just a few years after his tragic accident, and I find it just as moving, gracefully written, poignant, and, in many places, as amusing as his fiction.

I am sure that Andre was asked innumerable times during the sixteen years between *Separate Flights* and *Broken Vessels* why he bothered to remain with a small, struggling independent house of uncertain future, no demonstrable wealth, and publishing machinery that was creaky at best and non-functioning at worst. I am equally certain that within that period he was made innumerable offers from other houses that would have lined his pockets with far more in the way of both guarantees and earned royalties than we were ever able to provide. That Andre spurned these advances probably came as no surprise to those who knew him, for he was a man of fierce and passionate loyalties. These loyalties were not even necessarily personal; many were institutional: to this small publishing house in Boston, to a small college in Bradford, to the Marines, whose motto "Semper Fidelis" could also be cut on Andre's headstone as a description of how he lived his life. When he did leave us for Knopf, which had made him a most generous offer at a time when he desperately needed the money, he did so with obvious regret, genuine affection, and my complete blessing.

For literary advice and counsel Andre relied heavily on Bill Goodman, our extremely capable and sympathetic editor for over ten years. Bill soon learned that he couldn't, and shouldn't, tamper with anything Andre wrote—right down to the commas—but that they could spend endless happy hours discussing whether or not something worked: a scene, a character, a transition. Bill had an infallible ear for words, phrases, or scenes that were even slightly out of tune, and Andre was an attentive listener. Bill never presumed to suggest the solution (Andre managed to find these on his own), but he was extremely adept at pointing out the weak spots. They made a good team, Bill acting out the role of the congenial and professional editor, and Andre playing his part as the writer. I think all of his books were better for the collaboration.

For my own part, my personal encounters with Andre were limited but memorable. I once invited him to our island retreat off the coast of Maine, a place of few amenities and absolutely no nightlife. Andre spent the weekend running through the woods in his shorts, returning exhausted and devoured by small biting insects. He'd down entire six packs of beer, and then go out for another run to work it off. Evenings were spent regaling us with outrageous stories. I have never seen more beer consumed in my life. After his accident, I visited him a number of times in his small Haverhill home, often in the company of his children. We shared the felicity of naming our daughters Madeline, and much of our time was devoted to recounting their respective idiosyncrasies and adventures. I never left feeling in the least depressed or sorry for him. A terrible tragedy had befallen the man, but he was going to make the best of it, and make his own peace with God. I think he struggled with this, probably more than I realized, but he never felt sorry for himself or tried to elicit the sympathies of others.

I think Andre always tried to see life, and the relationships that life holds for all of us, clearly and unsentimentally. His writing is never mushy or clouded by sentiment. This contrasted strongly with his own person-ality—he was *always* a sentimentalist, always rooting for the underdog, resolutely loyal to his friends, and in thrall to his family. His standards were high—in literature, in behavior, in relationships—and it was the standards that he set for himself that made him so uncompromising, so intractable, and so exciting. He was, in every way, a major author. And a mighty fine human being.

Founded in 1970, **David R. Godine, Inc.** is a small, independent publishing house located in Boston, Massachusetts, producing thirty titles per year in a variety of genres and maintaining an active reprint program. All of Andre Dubus' titles published by the firm are still in print.

William B. Goodman

An Editor's Salute

If editing is taken to mean what the *American Heritage Dictionary's* first pass at it says—"To prepare (written material) for publication or presentation, *as by correcting, revising or adapting*"—it does not fit my decade as Andre Dubus' editor. Its third pass—"To modify or adapt *so as to make suitable or acceptable . . .*"—falls further from the mark. Both these meanings reflect much common editorial practice and both reflect the notion that there are uniform standards, moral, social and probably grammatical to which writing is properly held. All three smack of rules to be enforced. Dubus would have none of this. He wasn't a rules man. His sense of self, his craft, his professionalism combined to give him room and full license to find and uncover himself and his characters. No easy task and always long in finding text good enough to print.

I met him first in manuscript in late summer 1979. I knew little about him save for the story "Adultery," which was a tale writers passed around among themselves. When I had told Paula Fox I was going to Godine and would work with Dubus, she told me how much she admired "Adultery." David Godine gave me the manuscript for the novella "Finding A Girl in America" to read on vacation with my wife at Wellfleet before reporting for work at Dartmouth Street and Commonwealth Avenue, Godine's crowded offices in the basement of a grand nineteenth century carcass of a building Henry James and William Dean Howells could have known.

Here's how it begins: "On an October night, lying in bed with a nineteen-year old girl and tequila and grapefruit juice, thirty-five-year-old Hank Allison gets the story." That first sentence assured me there was a story, fully formed, ready to roll. Finding "Adultery's" Hank Allison there put more edge on anticipation. The story was long, it stretched to novella length, and worked all the way through. When it was over, I found I'd picked up nothing that needed correction, no typos, factual error, bum grammar or awkward usage. That surprised me, since I assumed I was reading a draft, and said to myself it was something to talk to Dubus about. There was something more important, however, and that was that I couldn't credit Hank's howling fury over Monica's resort to abortion to rid herself of a pregnancy he'd caused. To me his anguish, so fully exposed, didn't seem what a late twentieth century man would feel. Most would feel relief, I thought, as would many equally modern women. Nothing so febrile on both sides. I put the script aside and went on with our vacation.

Back in Boston, some weeks later, when I told Dubus my misgivings about Hank's fury, he laughed. I don't remember whether this was face to face or on the phone. We did meet that fall but, chances are, it was later. I liked that laughter. For one thing it showed great confidence and suggested that Dubus was not about to rethink "Finding A Girl in America." I told myself to reread the story and see where I came out. Holding fast to the givens, accepting what the text delivered, I understood Dubus' confidence and however much I thought Hank overreacted, I understood now that the Hank in this story could explode as he did.

Filled out with ten more stories, the book, titled for its novella, was published to mixed reviews in 1980, its jacket graced on the front cover in its first printing with a beach picture of Andre's wife Peggy Rambach, her back to the shore facing the open ocean.

Early on I asked Dubus how he worked. A good subject and one he was prepared to tell me about. He worked a story through as many drafts as necessary, always counting the words in each draft, usually cutting back as the drafts went on, till he got a draft that didn't make him too uncomfortable. That done he'd read it into a tape recorder and play it back to hear how it *sounded*. Oral reality was important to him. It had to sound right, especially what his people said, and that might mean changes. When he was satisfied, it meant that his text had passed its oral test. How long he continued this practice, or whether he kept the tapes he made rather than erase them, I do not know.

A manuscript, produced by this process, hardly needed editorial attention to its texts. If a date, or name or place were wrong and you pointed it out, he was grateful and happily made the correction. He awaited copyediting like a Marine under siege, prepared for anything and expecting to have to fight. What was left after all this—flap and catalog copy, worrying a jacket design until it was right, keeping galley and page proof schedules going, sales meeting presentations (which sometimes included a visit from Dubus)—had to be done. These chores usually included other hands in the house. Over the years there were six more books, the last being the essay collection *Broken Vessels*, published in 1991, just after I left Godine, and with an acknowledging debt paying paragraph in its front matter. Here he responds to the great flood of sympathy that washed over the Dubuses after the accident that made him a cripple and gave him a new subject. "Cripple" is his word. He used it when necessary like a club to expose the sentimentally empty. Some cripple!

> I am abidingly grateful to Ann Beattie, E.L. Doctorow, Gail Goodwin, John Irving, Stephen King, Tim O'Brien, Jayne Anne Phillips, John Updike, Kurt Vonnegut, and Richard Yates. On five Sunday afternoons in the winter of 1987, they read from their work at the ballroom of the Charles Hotel in Cambridge, Massachusetts, to raise money for me and my family, after I was struck by a car and lost a leg. And I am grateful to all those people who came to the benefit and to those who mailed checks to me in the year following my injury, and to Scott Donaldson and Frieda Arkin. All of this kindness saved me from financially going under, and made me feel, during a very bad time, that I had hundreds of friends I didn't even know.

Dubus thought of himself as a short story writer. That was the way he enclosed everything and got through it. Sometimes a story would grow into a novella. Now, a novella is not a novel nor meant to be. Dubus and I would sometimes talk about the difficulty of getting a technically satisfactory definition of the short story or novella / short novel. He was a master of the novella, and though a seasoned teacher of fiction at Bradford College, he didn't worry the definition question. It was one of those abstract puzzles some literary intellectuals lick like a dry bone and something clearly less important to him than stories themselves. As for novels, they were obviously for other writers. His first book, *The Lieutenant* (Dial Press, 1967), a product of his time at the Iowa Writers' Workshop, was a novel. Though he let himself be persuaded by a friend to allow a paperback reprint of it in 1986 by The Green Street Press, he preferred to forget it. He thought it a failed book because the novel as a form was not natural to his respiration as a writer. Thorough readers of his books are entitled to say, "But *Voices From The Moon* (1984) was published as a novel!" Well, yes, but Dubus can't be blamed for that curiosity. I had the book cast off in a format that got it to 126 numbered pages, enough to allow a small book that could be practically list priced and—may Chekhov forgive me!—got Dubus to let the front of the jacket say "A Novel By Andre Dubus." That small travesty did not tarnish the tale itself. It is included, please note, in his *Selected Stories* (1988).

I miss the focused immensity of his talent, the way he cultivates his chosen ground, and visit him now and then in some of his victories: "Adultery," "Waiting," "A Father's Story," "On Charon's Wharf." There are more. You pick them and so help him say his prayers.

William B. Goodman, a semi-retired editor/agent, lives in Bedford, Massachusetts.

Amy Schildhouse Greenberg

Lessons

Above all, Andre was my teacher. I valued his friendship, loved his soft *hello darlin'* Louisiana drawl, laughed at his diehard flirtatiouness, respected his prowess as a short story writer and essayist, but it is Andre the teacher whom I think I'll miss the most.

Like many of his admirers, I knew Andre's stories before I knew him. His work spoke loudly to me about real people: down-to-earth, imperfect folk who make mistakes and who savored the good life when it came their way. I always wanted to eat the grilled steaks and drink the gin and tonics in a Dubus story, or, like one of his characters, stretch my muscles after a good, sweaty run.

I learned from Andre that real writers lived anywhere. Although I met him when I worked for a large publisher in New York City, Andre taught me that not Manhattan, but places like Haverhill, Massachusetts, or Rogers City, Michigan, or even Columbus, Ohio, were the places where writers lived. He taught me—writers' conferences be damned—it wasn't who you knew, but what you knew that made you a writer.

From Andre I learned about generosity. Generosity to everyone, but specifically to other writers, especially younger or less accomplished ones in need of encouragement to *listen to what their hearts told them,* as Andre used to say.

And technical lessons, of course: the search for Flaubert's *mot juste,* not just any old word but the perfect word, for each sentence of one's story. Or using all five senses in every paragraph, or revising out loud. And many other lessons he probably never knew he was teaching. Andre taught me that most of the writers whose work I loved—like him— retained a childlike quality, a closeness to their childhoods that they never jettisoned. Andre was an old soul, but he was also as naive as a child, his needs stripped bare for all to see, trusting and wide open. A hard way to travel through everyday life, but essential for the writer he was.

The best writing, I learned from Andre, is not about artifice at all. It's not about constructing a literary voice, but rather about letting one's own voice be heard through one's characters. To me the narrator of a Dubus story always sounds, quite simply, like Andre talking. And the voice heard in one of his stories is usually a moral voice. Andre made me see that stories are as much about making moral choices as they are about recounting a good tale. Life is complex in a Dubus story or essay, but it is also very simple. There is a formula: you try your hardest to be a good person, trust God, make sure your actions mirror your values.

Andre taught me to stand by my work. Once I told him of a story I'd written about the rape of a white woman by a black man, a story which was demolished by my writers' workshop. "It's racist," the workshop leader pronounced. "No one will ever publish it." Andre asked me if I believed it was a good story. I told him that I did. He said that I should trust my instincts and, by the way, send him a copy of it to read. A few days later he telephoned. "Your story is true," he told me. "Emotionally true. I wouldn't change a line." Then he asked to include it in the anthology he was editing.

Write about what matters to you, Andre taught, and he did so himself, again and again. I tried to incorporate his lessons into my work as a visiting Writer-in-the-Schools. Last fall, I led a writing workshop for a class of ten-year-old writers. I asked them to list their three happiest and three saddest experiences. In other classes, this exercise had resulted in some fine stories. *Write about what matters to you,* Andre had said. I was particularly curious to read what one young girl might write. I knew that her mother, a neighbor of mine, was fighting a lengthening battle with cancer. Naively, I thought that writing a story about it might provide a sort of outlet or solace for the girl. The child, however, refused to complete the exercise. "I only like to write stories that are make-believe," she insisted.

Several months later, on an unseasonably warm afternoon in mid-February, I looked out my living room window to see that young girl's mother walking past my house, leaning heavily on the arm of a friend. I noticed how slowly she moved, how much effort each step cost her. Suddenly I understood her daughter's insistence on make-believe stories. I wanted to call Andre, to tell my teacher of this lesson I had learned on my own, but I didn't call immediately and then I never got the chance because he was gone.

This essay first appeared in "Remembering Andre," *StoryQuarterly 35.* Copyright © 1999 by Amy Schildhouse Greenberg. Reprinted by permission of the author.

Amy Schildhouse Greenberg's essay, "Dinners with Andre" was published by *Indiana Review* and nominated for a Pushcart Prize.

M.M.M. Hayes

A Workingman

I remember Andre Dubus most for a deceptive simplicity—a directness that upstaged all his contradictions: a great furry bear of a man,
physical even in his wheelchair; lusty and devout, salty and ethereal in
the same moment; despairing over the loss of his legs, then rising to
become a champion of the disabled. He taught so many of us with his
common sense and his strong heart. I first met Andre in a workshop he
conducted at the Indiana Writers' Conference in the summer of 1986—
three weeks before his accident. Andre opened by asking not only our
names but also something real and tangible about each of us—details he
didn't forget. He used them—on a need to know basis—to exalt the
humble, to knock down the arrogant: a well-executed blitz. I had never
encountered such an intense workshop experience. Andre led us full
throttle, conducting the weeklong workshop on a non-sleep basis. Our
2:00-4:00 p.m. class regularly went on until 6:00 p.m., then Andre
decamped and led us to a Bloomington blue-collar bar and pizza joint—
not to the nearby student hang-out, an important distinction for this
man who often referred to himself as a workingman. Finally, about the
fourth workshop, he led off with a *Whoof* and, "If this thing lasted three
more days, we'd all be in pajamas."

With Andre's permission, I taped one of these workshops and, in hindsight, one comment stands out, suggesting both the physical and spiritual Andre. He related an incident he'd heard, about another ex-marine:

> He always ran right into the crises whether he could do any-
> thing about them or not. And my friend [Andre's]—who had
> been taught this [behavior] in a psych class—said, "Y'know, it's
> nothing. It's just an example of training overcoming instincts.
> He didn't know what he was supposed to do when he got there.
> He just knew there was trouble and you go on through it."

Andre could have been describing himself, three weeks later, as he stood that night, in the middle of a dark, rain-slick road trying to help two injured people. That was Andre. As he once commented on a student story:

> Reminded me of "The Death of Iván Ilých," by Tolstoy. The only one who could console the dying Iván was a serf. Iván called for the man to massage his leg, at night. And that's about as comforting a story, as far as, I think, a love of all humanity— particularly by the serf for the dying Iván Ilých. Somebody's hurt, you love their leg. That's all.

There was so much more, of course. Andre spoke of his own conscience:

> For instance, because I grew up in the South when it was segregated, I still have incredible southern guilt, although I was raised by good parents. We did not say *nigger*. A Christian brother in sixth grade slapped a kid, fully enough to knock the shit out of him, because he said *nigger*. When he stopped blooding [Andre's word], this little brother picked up . . . you know those school desks, with all the books in the bottom? . . . this little brother picked up the desk, turned over the books, and said to the kid, *Now pick up those books*, WHACK! And they said we were sissies . . . . I've never gotten over the guilt of being white.

Andre was saying this in 1986, but he still thought of himself as South- ern, for he said,

> I don't know if it's true but I've always thought it was an irrel- evant question, the one about why there were so many of us writers in the South. The usual answer is, *There's a tradition of storytelling*. Bullshit. Any workingman's bar in America you go to, people communicate by telling stories.

At the opening of that first workshop, Andre laid out the rules, not as an exercise in power (well, maybe a bit), but as an exercise in leadership, because truly he led us, a pied piper playing his high-energy, running commentary—nipping discussion to the left, when the class didn't like a story:

I found her maneuver to be interesting. And his. I found them both to be insincere, dishonest with each other and they should never had been naked in the same room together, unless they were unconscious and stripped of their clothing by an outside force. If they're not intimate enough, even at dinner, to ever make love, then they shouldn't be together. I don't like either of the characters. I couldn't spend any time with them, but I like the *story*. It's a couple of assholes being assholes to each other and that's a pretty good subject and I thought this was a real story.

Or tucking us to the right, when we got too technical:

You can write a great novel that is empty and get away with it. American novels are not, generally, by my favorite writers. One, *From Here to Eternity*, had so many flaws and cracks you cannot read the story. But his [James Jones'] love of his characters and his passion take over. So much that the contrived parts, the awkwardness, the clumsiness don't matter. Don't matter. Take over the story.

When a student said one story was a good idea, Andre countered,

To say a story's a good idea doesn't mean anything. Everyone I know has good ideas. They're going to come to you and say, I've got a good idea for you, and you, you can tell 'em, you take your good idea and put it where the moon don't shine. Because an idea's nothing.

What was? Certainly braving the risk of loving people, certainly being the best Catholic he could muster, being a marine his fellows could depend on. But ultimately—as seen story by story in our workshop—Andre came back to personal honesty, the courage to go further and ask the hard questions, to find the trouble. He wielded fiction as flagellation, if you will, using factual events to butt into risk, to strip down events until the truth was bare. At one point, he said:

There's a time in a person's life when you should no longer be shocked. My mother was *shocked* for too long and . . . she maintained . . . *blindness* . . . because shock means: "Don't tell me that!" And there should be a time when we love life enough that we should face all of it and know that any old shit might come heading down the mountain.

Which is what happened, three weeks later. Andre was going to "see trouble and go right on through it." The crumpled motorcycle became one tong of a pincher action that seemed inevitable—the oncoming car rounding the blind curve and pinching off this great trumpet of a man. The following year, Andre sent me the original typewritten story in which he used my maiden and married names as the name of his character: Mitchell Hayes. He signed it, "Written in January 1987, at home in Haverhill, Massachusetts; the first story I wrote after being hit by a car on 23 July 1986, my daughter Cadence, then 4, was in the room with me when I finished it."

The first time I heard Andre read, he chose "A Father's Story" and, unlike many in that audience, I hadn't read it yet. But there, I thought, was the voice of a man who had mentioned his own children so often in class and, as I listened, I thought, *he's not going to turn his daughter in to the police. He's just not going to do it. So where is he going with this?* Then halfway through . . . seven-eighths of the way through the story, I thought: *this is not a man who can turn in his own daughter. He won't. If he does, I won't believe him, if he doesn't I already knew he wouldn't, so how's he going to get out of this?*

But then—my God, who could have been prepared—the human Andre, flawed and humbled, turned his back to us all, taking his case directly to God himself . . . and truly, the hair stood up along my arms and scalp as I heard him ascend with a roar, leaving behind him a trail of sparks and rainbow colors. Ah, there was a life.

M.M.M. Hayes' fiction has appeared in *New Stories from the South*, in *2Plus2, an International Anthology*, and *Best of the West*. Her stories have won a Katherine Anne Porter Prize from *Nimrod* and prizes from *Redbook Magazine*. She is Editor & Publisher of *StoryQuarterly*.

Thomas E. Kennedy

The Sharer

I met Andre Dubus by chance in Julio's bar in Montpelier, Vermont, the summer of 1984. I was a student in the M.F.A. program at Vermont College, and I didn't know who Andre was, but I had twenty dollars I had just earned for my first story sale—to a magazine named *Confrontation*—and I knew that he and the guy he was sitting with, Gordon Weaver, were writers, so I asked if they would help me drink up my honorarium. They graciously accepted. The twenty dollars did not last long, but we kept going nonetheless.

In the course of our conversation, I slowly began to realize that Andre Dubus was no ordinary writer, and somehow I figured out that in fact he was the author of a short story I had read in *The Best American Short Stories* fourteen years before, a marvelous fiction entitled "If They Knew Yvonne," which had been wonderfully liberating for me. The story is about a young man who, after years of pain and shame, finally figures out that it is not sex but the misuse of other human beings that is sinful; he tells this to the priest in confession and receives as a penance the instruction to say "Hallelujah!" three times.

It was well into the wee hours when I made the connection between that story and the man I was sharing strong drink with—perhaps we had already gone on to Charlio's, or The Thrush, or back to his rented house to drink his beer and eat his food, which we did more than once that summer. Wherever, delighted and amazed to learn he was Yvonne's creator, I felt I should do something to commemorate this chance meeting. So I asked Andre if he would be willing to allow me to interview him. He agreed. We did it by mail between Massachusetts and Denmark—where I live—over the next many months. I got hold of and read everything he had published up to that time and then composed a list of one hundred and eighteen questions. I wrote them one to a page, figuring that he could just type or write his replies right on the pages themselves, beneath the questions. This was before the time of the personal computer.

However, what Andre did was to sit down with a tape recorder and talk into it so that I got a "real" interview, spontaneous, funny, insightful, and fun. He devoted a good many hours to answering those questions, even the blundering ones. In the end I wound up with six tape cassettes. When I transcribed them onto paper, I had a typescript of over a hundred pages—which ultimately provided a good part of the basis for my first published book, *Andre Dubus: A Study of the Short Fiction*.

That was the kind of guy Andre was. A sharer. He would share with you his food, his drink, his time, his contacts, and his wisdom.

This essay first appeared in "Remembering Andre," *StoryQuarterly 35*. Copyright © 1999 by Thomas E. Kennedy. Reprinted by permission of the author.

Thomas E. Kennedy's most recent story collection is *Drive, Dive, Dance & Fight*. His collection of essays on the craft of fiction, *Realism and Other Illusions*, has just been published. Kennedy's *Andre Dubus: A Study Of The Short Fiction* was published by Twayne/Macmillan in 1988.

Kacey Kowars

Letters from Andre

I don't remember much about the fall and winter of 1983; I spent most of it trying, unsuccessfully, to stop drinking. I flew to New York on New Year's Eve and checked into The Hotel Blackstone on 58th Street. I was in the midst of a profound bout of self-pity, unwilling to recognize that the bottle of beer I held in my hand was killing me. The man staring back at me in the bathroom mirror was a stranger, but a man, nonetheless, that I knew well. I did what I always did to dam the flow of self-pity. I took a drink.

Ten days later, on January 10, 1984, I checked into St. Anthony's Hospital for the third time. The doctors and the nurses explained to me, in no uncertain terms, that if I continued to drink I would die. I decided I wanted to live.

I turned to books for solace, turned to them with a fierceness that has never abated. I continued praying, but I found myself opening a book when the need to meditate struck me.

A miracle occurred during that dismal winter of 1984. I was browsing in a small independent bookstore in Bexley, Ohio, looking for something interesting to read. I spotted a book on the shelf titled *The Times Are Never So Bad* by Andre Dubus. I picked up the book and examined it, opening its pages to smell its print. On the back of the dust jacket Frederick Busch had written,

> This powerful collection is about crimes, large and small, and about our clumsy and heart-rending efforts to forgive one another our inevitable trespasses. The writing is direct, compassionate and wise. The characters are bent beneath a weight that Andre Dubus, one feels, would bear for them if he could—their utter plausible and undefended humanness, the terrible freight that children and parents carry to each other. In "A Father's Story,"

the brilliant completion of the book, Dubus reveals himself to be not only a prophet of the roadhouse, but an honest *religious* writer: a most important American voice.

The book's title comes from Saint Thomas More, who wrote, "The times are never so bad but that a good man can live in them." The novella and stories that follow, were the best short fiction I'd ever read. It was if Dubus had been following me around and taking notes on my weaknesses.

Later that year I was in the same bookstore when I saw another book written by Dubus—*Voices from the Moon.* The book was a mere 126 pages long, and something about its size appealed to me. I read it in one sitting.

In one of the book's most poignant scenes, Larry talks with his mother, Joan, at the restaurant where she works. He tells her of the pain he feels when he sees his father with Brenda, Larry's ex-wife. Joan eases her son's mind by telling him what he already knows, that one day he will forgive his father and Brenda; that they will learn to live with the changes.

> "You know why I like my waitress friends so much? And what I have learned from them?" Joan asks Larry. "They don't have delusions. So when I'm alone at night—and I love it Larry—I look out my window, and it comes to me: we don't have to live great lives, we just have to understand and survive the one's we've got."

This sentence loosened something inside me, unlocked a secret door that had been too long closed. I took out a pencil and paper and wrote Andre Dubus a letter. I told him of my life and of the changes I had recently made. I told him how important his work was to me. I told him I was giving his book as a Christmas present to my friends, urging them to discover what I had found in his writing. I sent the letter to David Godine, his publisher, in Boston. I had never written a letter to an author before. I did not expect a reply from Dubus.

Months passed. I continued working and not drinking; slowly things began to get better. I made it through Christmas and New Year's. Then, on February 8, 1985, I opened the mailbox to find a solitary envelope. I looked at the letter. It was hand-addressed to me. In the left-hand corner of the envelope I saw Andre Dubus' name. I sat down at the table. My hands were shaking.

February 5, 1985

Hello Kacey,

I feel terrible. You wrote a wonderful and encouraging letter and it came at a time when I had lost my ritual, and also my discipline. I'm an awful correspondent and my friends have given up on me. After writing fiction, I simply cannot bring myself back to the desk that day. But I came up with a means to at least give respect to readers who write: I keep on hand post cards, and try to answer a reader as soon as I've read the letter.

However your letter arrived while we were en route to New York to visit my wife's family. My wife read it to me in the car. Three weeks before that we had moved to a house we built—had built—our first one. I had recently retired from teaching, and there was much suppressed emotion there. I was working on, hanging onto a novella that I have now finished. I know little of its worth, but I know from my fatigue and post-partum depression that it is the most intense long story (80 pp) I've done. Seems that Godine will publish it with two others in 1986. So what I was doing during that time of the move, and retiring, was trying each day to work. I didn't even exercise, and normally I work out for an hour a day six days a week. This is an important ritual to me. I still don't feel entirely at home in my new house— can't find things. But I've been walking a lot in the woods, hunting rabbits without success, and trying to regain peace of soul. This is a long apology/ excuse and one you deserve.

Your letter deeply touched me. I'm also deeply touched that you gave my little book to friends. So far I've been lucky with booze. I obviously love to drink, but mostly a relaxing buzz in front of the VCR at the end of the day, or a stimulating buzz with friends at a bar. I'm physically blessed: I have never been able to consider the hair of the dog next day. My remedy for a real hangover is a long workout, a lazy shower, then perhaps a nap. Then two martinis, a solid meal with wine, and go to bed with a detective novel.

I'm so happy that you say I've touched your life. I screw up so much with people I love. Certainly you have touched my life.

All best to you, blessings,

Health, love, and peace

Andre

Twelve years have passed since that cold February evening, but the thrill of opening that letter has never diminished. I read the letter over and over again until I had it memorized. I sat in the comfort of my living room and drank black coffee.

Not only had Andre responded to my letter, he shared a part of his life with me. He told me that my letter had "touched his life." Although I had been an avid reader for years, this was the first time I truly understood the power of writing, the impact the simple act of putting pencil to paper can have. I re-read *Voices from the Moon*.

I have been reluctant to show Andre's letter to people; it feels too personal to keep on display. But not a minute has passed since its arrival when I have not known exactly where the letter is.

I first heard of Dubus' accident on National Public Radio. Information was difficult, if not impossible, to come by. A year passed and I wrote him the first of a series of encouraging letters, telling him there was a man in Ohio who needed him to write fiction again when he was able. I offered him my prayers. I felt helpless. I continued writing Andre letters, assuring him I did not expect a response.

During the period between 1987-1990 I discovered the writings of James Lee Burke. I read *The Neon Rain* and *Heaven's Prisoners* with the same sort of admiration with which I read Dubus.

In 1990 I read in *The New York Times* that Godine would be publishing a collection of Dubus' essays titled *Broken Vessels*. The collection would combine some of Andre's earlier essays with a group of essays he wrote chronicling his recovery from his accident. The essays are brilliant and revealing, and, as always with Andre's writing, painstakingly honest.

I bought the book the day it was published. I wrote Andre, to tell him that *Broken Vessels* sat in a position of honor on my bookshelf. I also told him of my admiration for James Lee Burke's writing.

November 23, 1991

Hello, Kacey,

James Lee Burke is my first cousin. We spent every summer together, from the age of 5 till manhood. Thank you deeply, my friend, for your beautiful and strengthening letters. And for your prayers. And for sharing the heart-breaking story of your father. BROKEN VESSELS actually interrupted my life—that hasn't happened before—and I got way behind on mail.

Many thanks,
Andre

1992 and 1993 were dark years for me. I went through a painful divorce, and I lost virtually everything I had worked for except my sobriety and my love of books. I ended up selling most of my rare-book collection to make ends meet. I wrote Andre a letter in the winter of 1993 and I gave him my new address in Columbus.

February 2, 1994

Hello, Kacey:

I'm sorry about your divorce. I feel soiled by mine and have nothing good to say about them. One day at a time is right. I hope Columbus serves you well. I greatly appreciate your kind words and, even more, your prayers.

God bless you,
Andre

I lost another job later that year. I wrote to Andre in the summer and told him that I had found a new job and that things were looking up. I told him I was dating a woman from Indianapolis, my first romantic experience since my divorce.

August 21, 1994

Hello, Kacey:

I am very happy to hear you are dating. I certainly think it's good to risk love again. You've been through enough suffering, and ought to seek peace and fullness, if she smiles at you.

I was lucky with booze: it didn't bite me the way it bit you and Cousin Jimmy. I'm very proud of Jimmy, for staying sober, staying married, staying a father and a writer. I pray that you'll stay sober too.

It's awful that you lost two jobs. It seems the heart has gone out of a lot of organizations, maybe a lot of people too. And these rich ball players won't play for us. Yesterday, at a family party to celebrate my birthday and my oldest daughter's, a friend said: "What ever happened to shame?" He was talking about the ballplayers.

I recommend to you Reynolds Price's A WHOLE NEW LIFE, about his cancer and crippling. It's not about divorce, alcohol, and losing jobs, but it's a spiritual and—I think—a soothing book for anyone who suffers or who has suffered.

I shall keep you in my prayers. I am grateful I am in yours. I have a story appearing in SEWANEE REVIEW'S fall issue, a story sometime in EPOCH. I signed with Knopf so I could pay for my house, contracts for a book of stories and a book of essays. I'm about one story short in the book of stories.

Peace and Love,
Andre

The book of stories he referred to in his letter would be published as *Dancing After Hours* in 1996. One of the stories in the collection, "Woman on a Plane," was in the fall 1995 issue of *Ploughshares*. It was the first new fiction of Dubus' that I had read in nearly a decade. The story is about a young woman who has a brother dying from AIDS, a brother "dying from love."

When I read this story I had recently attended the funeral of a good friend of mine who had died from AIDS, the first such loss I had suffered. I will always be grateful to Andre for giving me the beautiful simplicity of that sentence. Suddenly I knew why Jerry had died. I could cast the ugly words I had been using aside. After finishing the story, I wrote Andre.

October 14, 1995

Hello, Kacey:

It's good to hear from you again. I finished my book and took most of the summer off; haven't done that since boyhood. Wrote a little, watched a little baseball and movies, swam a lot, hung out with the family. I believe I failed to answer your last letter before this one. I'm sorry; once I leave the desk it takes a threat to get me to write again that day. But every morning I pray for you. I'm glad you haven't given up on love. All the best with your book.

Love,
Andre

The book he mentions is a biography on the life of Walter Tevis I had been working on. I told him that my relationship with the woman from

Indianapolis was winding down, but that I was not giving up on love. At first I was reluctant to share my sorrows and disappointments with a man who had suffered the way Andre had, but I have learned the importance of being rigorously honest with those I love and care for. There is no other way—for how can you share your joys if you have not shared your sorrows as well? Damaged people have always freely offered me their solace, have always provided a safety net.

Finally, in March of 1996, Knopf published *Dancing After Hours* to rave reviews. Andre was awarded the Rea Prize for fiction, an award rarely given, signifying mastery of the short story form.

I wrote Andre and told him how much I enjoyed the stories, and how proud I was of him for having the courage to write fiction again. I enclosed some writing tips by Walter Tevis that I knew Andre would like. I told him my life was getting back on track and that for the first time in years I felt hope.

April 5, 1996

Hello, Kacey:

Good to hear from you. Good work with your writing. I enjoyed the writing tips. Each morning I pray for you.

God bless. Love,
Andre

It suddenly hit me that Andre Dubus prayed for me and had been praying for me for years. Somehow the thought of his prayers made me realize that everything that had been bothering me would work itself out, that I was not in control of life's mysteries.

During 1997 my fortunes improved. I began to collect rare books again, buying back many of the titles I had sold in 1993. In March I purchased a small collection from a friend of mine who knew of my love of book collecting. The collection included writers like Carson McCullers, Thornton Wilder, John Hersey, William Gaddis, and Ernest Hemingway.

One of the books was Hemingway's collection from 1927, titled *Men Without Women*. The copy I bought had no dust jacket, the only such book in my collection. I hate to admit how much this bothered me. The only reason the book stayed on my shelf was the fact that it was a first edition and that Hemingway had written it. So there the book stayed—safe, but different from the others.

In April of 1997 Andre published an essay titled "A Hemingway Story" in the spring issue of the *Kenyon Review*. The essay discusses the short story "In Another Country," and Andre writes of how his accident altered his reading of the story, how he now understood the role physical pain played in the story.

The next day I sent my copy of *Men Without Women* to Andre.

28 May 97

Hello Kacey:

Thank you, thank you, thank you—I have never owned a hardcover copy of MEN WITHOUT WOMEN. What a book! I had not known—or had forgotten—that he was so young when he wrote "In Another Country." And the others. I treasure the book, and your friendship, your prayers.

I was also excited by your article about the very interesting artist in the magazine you sent me. You're a good writer, and I wish you well with your novel. I am plagued with a root canal now, and the medication, but I wanted to write you as soon after receiving your gift as I could.

I have finished my book of essays, had two grandsons—27 March and 7 April—and may be falling for a girlfriend.

You are in my morning prayers.

Love,
Andre

I sat by myself with a cup of coffee and savored the miracle of books and their writers.

Kacey Kowars has been a stockbroker for twenty-one years. He has recently completed *The Money Game*, the first in a series of Wall Street mysteries. He lives in Columbus, Ohio with his wife, Tina Rich, and his stepdaughter, Brittany Sharnsky.

Kai Maristed

The Measure Given

"Sounds like your best route will be straight up 495, past the Lowell Connector, through Lawrence. Haverhill's big, there's four exits. You wait for the last one. About when you come off the ramp right, the sun will be setting over your left shoulder. . . ." So ran Andre's instructions to a total stranger, on how to get to his home and into his life. Home, because that's where he hosted a small gang of novice writers one night a week. Life, because the subject was writing.

"Maybe you'd like to come up next Thursday, see if we're anything you'd like to be part of?" His gallant form of invitation, issued over the phone in a husky, roaring accent (Louisiana, Marine Corp drill deck, blue collar North Shore) that I had to strain to comprehend. After three months' silence, this was his response to a few rough chapters sent to him by the stranger, who was then not so much an admirer of Dubus' oeuvre as an eager writing fool. A pest without any claim.

At the outset he had apologized, "I'm sorry I took so damn long to answer your letter. I was recovering from an accident. Kind of slowed me up." Then with no further preamble he launched into a quiz about my characters. So why did Cherry do this instead of that? Were the parents dead or alive? Most of all, did I have a map for where this story was going? Forbidden, un-"literary" questions. *Reader's* questions. I stammered and sweated bullets. At that moment, nine-thirty p.m., in the fall of 1987, a guy whom I had yet to meet knew his way around my work better than I did.

The group was still new when I joined, probably an experiment by someone who loved teaching and could not teach at the local college anymore. (Later his close friend Jack would say, *he needs you guys more than you need him.*) About eight or nine of us gathered in from a wide radius. Scatter of cars tipped in what still were hayfields. Sunsets in Haverhill, that year and for the next three, were slow and languorous, blinding orange to lush rose to indigo. We lugged sacks of beer and snacks zigzag up the wheelchair ramp. Often a pot of chili or gumbo bubbled in the cramped kitchen, and anyone caught short of drink was encouraged to help himself from the fridge. After some palaver we sat down in two facing rows—some with backs to the long picture window, others facing the mesmerizing changes of the sunset. Andre parked his movable chair on the eastern end, where he could see the faces in both rows. In his leather satchel the necessities: notebook, pencil, pills, Zippo, pack of Gauloises or Schimmelpennincks. (He aspired to purely working-class pleasures, but a few refinements had snuck in.) I'd jump to fetch the forgotten ashtrays—most of us still smoked, back then. Jake, Andre's senior golden retriever, would thump his ribcage down on the wood floor and proceed to wheeze through the evening. Later there was no more Jake, and Andre only dreamed and wrote about him.

Bro Jack, who shared the house then, usually took the space opposite Andre, filling the far end of what seemed like an invisible long table. As if we were a family. We did argue, yell, weep, and laugh together like one.

Nothing was closed off, nothing hidden. The kitchen door was never locked. If I arrived early Andre might shout my name with a question mark from his bedroom. Then I'd walk down the corridor past the daughters' rooms and find him in the struggle of arranging himself—the leg-and-a-third, the clothing—while he talked about what was most on his mind. One of his sons or daughters, often. His physical frustrations. The Red Sox. A fear. That he shared his troubles was one form of Dubus' generosity.

There was no danger, in his case, of confusing "generous" with "good" (whatever that is exactly) nor with "kind." He was not always particularly kind. His raunchy joking could humiliate a girl. He and I clashed over the Tao of deer hunting, morality of abortion, the limits of patriotism. He drove some people away from our (growing and shifting) Thursday group with razor-edged, passionate or just plain disgusted reactions to the work they had just read—and those so injured did not go quietly into the Haverhill night. There were dramas, and aftershocks. We who stayed received our fair share of cuts, wounds to suck and ponder on. But not enough to make us, for a single moment, want to leave.

A random grab from the good things he opened up for me: The Cowboy Junkies, Rebecca Parris' ballads, the stories of Susan Dodd, Tobias Wolff and Richard Yates, extraordinary friendships, joke-telling, how to read Chekhov, what it means to be no longer a biped, how it feels to hold a gun, Catholicism.

He didn't mind sharing his animosities either: the yuppified TinaBrowned *New Yorker*, status-y writing utensils (once I haplessly pulled a $14 metallic Cross pen from my bag: *a fuckin' New Yorker pen!* he choked), the usurious sin of "name" authors who charged money for their teaching (less, surely, than we got for free)—money, and obsequiousness. One Manhattan tyrant refused to let his students go to the can during the hours-long sessions. *What kind of pussies put up with that?*

His responses to our work, for all the risk of ego-bruising, were beyond price. He could listen. (We did not hand around texts. He swore by the sound and rhythm of the writing.) Later he plucked out details—*you got the shape of the boy's teeth in the kiss, I* like *that, and that word, "twilight", s'beautiful, can be a beginning or an end*—in a way that made hardboiled writers go numb with pleasure. But what he was mainly listening for was "what's stirring here, what this story wants to *be*," and he encouraged us all to ferret, dig, labor for that thing at the heart—an emotion, relationship, insight—which generally turned out to be radically different from whatever the writer had first assumed he or she was up to. His gift lay not so much in articulating hunches that were (in my memory at least) uncannily on target, as in showing us that a real story may lurk in the awkwardest beginning, and that like a poem a story is never finished, only, after years of exploration, laid aside.

He wasn't the boss. He did not initiate or manipulate the discussion. He laid his own writing bare, reading from his starts, from his notebook. He revealed how he worked, or tried to, his "tricks"—extracting plots from newspaper stories, for example. He wanted *our* raw reactions and got them. He could be hurt and could hurt himself. He tore pages out of his notebook, hissing, "*Riffs*, nothing but goddamn stupid riffs going nowhere—" For a dismal, terrible time he feared he would never write fiction again.

We were not limited to Thursday nights with Andre. Even after I phased out—for everything has its right ending—there were his August birthdays and periodically a wedding or reading or someone's book to celebrate (by now almost all of us have seen the chilly light of publication) and our Haverhill Christmas parties with Secret Santa mischief. We felt big in his life. But compared to his children, to old friends, peers of enormous talent? Nor were we even the *only* group. He also gave an evening workshop to troubled teenagers from the town. Sometimes, like a jealous kid, I wondered, Did he like them and their work better?

Not all writers act generously toward members of their own species. Andre, with casual grace, offered us who he was, and whatever he had on hand, and perhaps the most precious thing possible—distillations of what he'd learned about writing. I also happen to teach these days, drawing on the Haverhill memory account. He never held back. In that spirit, here's a taste of his gift:

Nobody forces us to write stories. We're volunteers.

How to see from the point of view of a girl, a Vietnamese soldier, someone older than you are? *It's why we have imagination.*

Keep dialogue to the minimum. Give only the lines *necessary* to the story.

Tell the background, don't show.

Where to start a story? At the moment when everything in your character's previous life converges—at the nick between past and future.

Kai Maristed's most recent book is the story collection, *Belong to Me.* She is currently working on a novel.

Joe Massa

Unforgettable Pal, Wondrous Writer

The last time I saw Andre, we were 10- or 11-year-old classmates. It was during the early postwar years of 1946 and 1947, and we were fifth-grade students at Cathedral, an all-boys' Catholic school in Lafayette. The hub of Acadiana was then a small town, a few years before the oil boom in the Gulf of Mexico would transform it into a small metropolis. In the 1940s and early 1950s, though, it was a place where most families knew every other family and friendships were easily fostered.

In school, Andre and I were always No. 1 and No. 2 respectively at the end of the academic year, much to the chagrin of my mother, who thought I should have been numero uno. But I always felt Andre was more learned than I, perhaps more intelligent than anyone else I knew.

Andre and I were not just classroom competitors but also playmates after school and on weekends. We lived only a block apart, he in a two-story mansion-like brick structure in a middle-class neighborhood on a street named Adrienne. It was a fascinating place for a little boy to visit because of all the stairs and because it had an inside garage that descended into the ground, a basement. That was most unusual for a home in Lafayette and a delight for a boy on a bike, in a wagon or on anything capable of rolling downhill.

Andre was also an avid moviegoer, as I was, and we wound up going to the cinema a lot in downtown Lafayette when the city had those grand movie palaces, the Jefferson and Azalea theaters, which were eventually razed to make way for "progress."

Andre also was a good soccer player, the game Cathedral officials encouraged us to play in the fields behind the school. Soccer was my favorite participatory sport, and I remember how much fun it was to rush down the grassy field with my friends and fellow classmates like Andre and, if given the chance, to land a solid kick to that ball. But when it came time for me to enter the sixth grade in September 1947, my parents switched me to the public school system because there was an elementary school much closer to my house. That was the last I saw of Andre. I made new acquaintances and started going to the homes of other friends. The loss of the school connection disengaged me from Andre as well as other friends from Cathedral.

In the years afterward, however, I was to know all about Andre and what became of him. I followed his illustrious career for decades, cheering him on to greater heights. And what heights he reached! Last Friday, I read his obituary in the *Times-Picayune* and also in *The New York Times*—a lengthy four-column spread at the top of the page, with picture, summarizing the life and career of Andre Dubus, 62, a prize-winning author celebrated for his short stories. The size of his obituary in the nation's preeminent newspaper affirms for history the importance of this Louisiana-bred writer's legacy in the literary arts. It is a fine testament to a wondrous writer I knew as a little boy.

He first came to my attention on the literary front when I was shopping in a New Orleans bookstore in the 1960s and the novel *The Lieutenant* caught my eye. Could its author be the person from my childhood? It was, and I eagerly purchased the novel and brought it home to read.

The book jacket gave a peek at the author's life up to then, including the fact that he grew up in Lafayette, attended McNeese State University in Lake Charles and spent 5½ years in the U.S. Marine Corps. That revelation really threw me for a loop because it seemed such an unlikely thing to do for the kid I once knew.

The Lieutenant was about a Marine Corps officer, and Dubus obviously got the idea while serving in the armed forces. Like most first novels by unknowns, it didn't make the best-seller list but it did launch him into the ranks of published writers. It was not until the 1970s that he became more noticeable, this time as a short story writer. If you purchased a copy of the annual *The Best American Short Stories*, you would almost always find Andre Dubus represented in the 20 or so stories selected. In fact, if you didn't find a Dubus short story in that anthology, it would have been newsworthy.

One of my favorite Dubus short stories selected as one of the year's best is "If They Knew Yvonne." The story reflected Dubus' upbringing in the Catholic school system. Here's a sampling:

> Waiting in line for my first confession in five months, I felt some guilt but I wasn't at all afraid. I only had to confess sexual intercourse, and there was nothing shameful about that,

nothing unnatural. It was a man's sin. Father Broussard warned me never to see this girl again (that's what he called her: this girl), for a man is weak and he needs much grace to turn away from a girl who will give him her body. He said I must understand it was a serious sin because sexual intercourse was given by God to married couples for the procreation of children and we had stolen it and used it wrongfully, for physical pleasure, which was its secondary purpose. I knew that in some way I had sinned, but Father Broussard's definition of that sin fell short and did not sound at all like what I had done with Yvonne. So when I left the confessional I still felt unforgiven.

Dubus called himself "a Catholic writer," and that was evident in his work. He also was called an American Chekhov, a master of the short story—high praise indeed. His work was always relevant to the issues of our times. As the *Times-Picayune* book editor Susan Larson wrote in her obituary of Dubus: "The life of the spirit was always a major concern in his work."

In 1986, Dubus was driving near Boston one night when he spotted two motorists in trouble on the roadside. His Good Samaritan instincts intact, he stopped to help. As we know, an oncoming car struck him, resulting in the amputation of one leg and the use of the other. He used a wheelchair for the rest of his life.

In 1992, Dubus' book *Broken Vessels*, which chronicled his ordeal after the accident, was a runner-up for the Pulitzer Prize. I wish he'd won. He was certainly deserving of the recognition. But I wished for other things for Andre, too. I wished he hadn't been on that Massachusetts road that night; I wished he was still able to play soccer as he did when we were kids. And I wished I had called him last fall.

Our travel editor, Millie Ball, had occasion to call Andre for a piece she was doing in her section. Knowing she was going to call him, I asked her to mention my name to see if Andre remembered me. She did and, boy, did he remember! Millie said Andre seemed to be cheered by the mention of my name and recounted how we went to the movies together and played to our heart's content.

Millie urged me to call Andre, but I procrastinated. And now it's too late. But, Andre, I'm glad I knew you in your early years, and I'm so proud of your success, which will live forever.

This article first appeared, in a slightly different form in The New Orleans *Times-Picayune* on March 4, 1999. Copyright © 1999 by Joe Massa. Reprinted by permission.

Joe Massa was, for many years, a writer for the *Times-Picayune*. He lives in Metairie, a suburb of New Orleans.

Charles E. May

Love of the Short Story

The pressure on writers by agents, editors, and critics to abandon the short story as soon as possible and do something serious with their lives—such as write a novel—is unrelenting. This narrative bias that bigger is better persists in spite of the fact that the faithful few who have ignored it are among the most critically acclaimed writers of the twentieth century: Anton Chekhov, Jorge Luis Borges, Flannery O'Connor, Peter Taylor, Alice Munro, Grace Paley, Raymond Carver. Andre Dubus, another one of these devotees of the "lonely voice," speaks for all of them honestly and concisely, as the form demands: "I love short stories because I believe they are the way we live." Because I too love short stories and have spent my academic life studying how they express the way we live, I offer this little appreciation as a tribute to Andre Dubus' mastery of that form.

Following the publication of *Dancing After Hours,* Dubus' first collection of stories after his accident—also, sadly, his last—he told an interviewer that his disability seemed to have increased his empathy. Asked if he had become a better writer after the accident, he said, "I hope so. That would be a blessing." The title story of the collection is a beautiful incarnation of that blessing and a model of how the short story illuminates the "way we live." Richard Bausch has said that Dubus demonstrates clearly why the short story is such a persistent form: "For the fact is that there are matters of the spirit the short story addresses better than any other literary art." Joining such exemplars of the form as Chekhov's "Gooseberries," Joyce's "The Dead," and Carver's "Errand," "Dancing After Hours" epitomizes the "matters of the spirit" that the short story makes its own.

"What I want and want to give," Dubus remarked once, "more than the intimacy of words, is shared ritual, the sacraments. I believe that, without those, all our talking, no matter how enlightened, will finally drain us, divide us into two confused and frustrated people, then destroy us as lovers." "Dancing After Hours" is one of Dubus' finest "shared rituals," a communion in which even as the characters—reflections of us all in our lonely and fragile flesh—transcend mere externalities through spiritual union. This is one of the great romantic themes of the short story since its beginning, a religious theme that originated in the early nineteenth century and has been illuminated brilliantly by the form up to the present day.

Emily Moore, the central character in "Dancing After Hours," a forty-year old bartender in a town in Massachusetts, has always wanted a pretty face, but has lacked "the mysterious proportion" of such; her belief that she was homely as a girl and a young woman has "deeply wounded her." This is not a trivial injury. Typical of the musical way the short story communicates matters of the spirit, all the characters in the story resonate with this theme. Kay and Rita, the other two waitresses, also live alone. Like the old waiter in Hemingway's "A Clean, Well-Lighted Place," Rita hates to go home alone. Emily knows that Kay is falling in love with Rita; she imagines her walking into her apartment, listening to her answering machine with both hope and dread.

Indeed, it is Emily's ability to imagine the secret lives of the other characters—which reflects Dubus' own ability to empathize—that makes the story such a communal triumph. At night when she cannot sleep, she reads and, like all readers, is opened to the world by the women, men, and children on the pages. In a wonderful echo of Joyce's "The Dead," Dubus says that though Emily's sorrow remains, she is consoled as she "became one with the earth and its creatures: its dead, its living, its living after her own death; one with the sky and water, and with a single leaf falling from a tree."

The theme of externals that separate and the spirit that unites is echoed in Emily's memory of the blind musician Roland Kirk, who in a small club twenty years before, told the crowd that it was nice coming to work blind: "Not seeing who's fat or skinny. Ugly. Or pretty." When he comes off the stage and puts his arm around Emily to dance, she understands what it is "to love without the limits of seeing; so to love without the limits of the flesh." When he hugs her, she does not feel like a woman in the embrace of a man; "she melded; she was music."

This is, of course, the brilliant central metaphor of the story—the dance, which, even as it is intensely physical, strives to transcend the physical, the dancer mysteriously dissolving into the dance itself. The skydive Drew tells about likewise embodies an effort to escape the deadly effect of gravity and transcend the body. And through all this communal sharing and memory there is the music: the singing of Frank Sinatra, the saxophone of Paul Desmond.

When I was in college in a small town in Eastern Kentucky in 1962, I went to hear the Dave Brubeck quartet at the University of Louisville with some friends; it was my first concert. I sat there entranced by the piano of Brubeck, and then this unearthly sound came from nowhere; it was not as if I heard it, but rather that it became part of my breathing; it was Paul Desmond, standing over to the side, blowing his horn as if he were doing nothing very special. While reading "Dancing After Hours" again recently, I got out my old undergraduate *Take Five* album, closed my eyes, and put myself back in that Louisville auditorium when everything dissolved.

I didn't have a copy of Frank Sinatra singing "Dancing in the Dark," but then, in a bit of romantic serendipity, my 16-year-old daughter— who, for God knows what mysterious reasons, has become a Sinatra fan— came home excited because she had found an armful of Sinatra albums in a thrift store—the treasured collection, according to the label on one of them, of Miss Mary A. Whalen, of 39 Cushman Road, Brighton, Mass. (Thank you, Mary. I hope you are well.) Among them was *Come Dance With Me*! on which Sinatra sings "Dancing in the Dark" with a swing rhythm; as Emily sings along, "We're waltzing in the wonder of why we're here," and Kay and Rita dance, I smile and reach out to take my daughter's hand.

Short stories revolve around their central theme as in a piece of music, repeating with variations. Jeff, the manager of the bar, still somewhat dazed after his wife of twenty-three years left him, tells Emily about a friend made a quadriplegic in Viet Nam; Jeff says the man knew that his body was his enemy and that when he fought it he lost. "What he had to do was ignore it. That was the will. That was how he was happy." Emily watches her "pretty friends" dance in a magical moment that is truly "after hours," as if time has stood still and no one wants it to start again. In the wee small hours of the morning, the group reluctantly separate, but not completely. Drew promises to return. Emily watches Rita drive away with Kay and feels tender and hopeful for them. Jeff and Emily make plans to go fishing and share a meal. In the end, which is a beginning, Emily reaches through the window and squeezes Jeff's hand.

"Then she drove east, smelling the ocean on the wind moving her hair."

I never knew Andre Dubus, except in the way that readers know writers who dare to explore mysteries of the spirit and secrets of the heart and share their discoveries. The greatest tribute a reader can pay to such a writer is to say, "I hope I understood. Thank you, Andre."

Charles E. May is editor of *Short Story Theories* and *The New Short Story Theories*.

James McConkey

The Moral Backbone of The Anatomy of Memory

Though it took some persuasion on the part of an editor at Oxford University Press, I agreed about ten years ago to assemble an anthology about memory. I was then almost seventy, about to become an emeritus professor, and close to the completion of the third and final volume of *Court of Memory*, an autobiographical account that I had begun during the early days of the Cold War as a means of expressing and communicating the values and meanings of ordinary life. My initial hesitation to undertake the anthology had nothing to do with the pressures of work, or of deadlines of any sort; rather, it was the consequence of the importance of the subject to me. I have been called a memoirist, but I don't think of myself as one. I became an autobiographical writer primarily because on one long-ago winter night I underwent a kind of conversion. As humans, we are normally so unaware—so flawed by habitual sight—that it takes the likelihood of imminent loss to make us conscious of the profound value of all that surrounds us. I don't remember what particular crisis existed that night, but nuclear annihilation was such a possibility that the living world suddenly became sacramental to me, its parts interconnected.

Such an inner experience is really beyond language, but still it gave me, at long last, a voice—a way, that is, of interpreting and organizing experience. Why should the world have suddenly become holy? Not just because our species seemed about to destroy itself, I think. Something else—was it in my genetic memory, in my very body, or was it a response from my childhood?—had contributed to that awareness. I can't relive that ephemeral moment, but I've had others enough like it to bring its recall and to reinforce my sense of the value underlying the ordinary and commonplace. Personal memory, that subjective interpretation of experience, is the key to identity and consciousness, and yet it works in ways beyond conscious control: at almost every instant in our lives, it is effortlessly connecting the present with the past, finding likenesses and analogies and emotional associations in its continual attempts at understanding. Liable as it is to error and distortion, memory seems always in search of a synthesis, or unity, beyond its normal power. Our tragedy, as a species, may also lie in our genetic heritage; for, through fright or phobia or some nationalistic or ethnic disease, we are apt to stop memory's search too soon by excluding others, by finding connections only in our own tight little group.

Now, memory is a vast subject, one that has been explored by theologians, philosophers, psychologists, and increasingly in our own time by neurobiologists; but what really matters most to me is its spiritual dimension, as the source of the desires that define the human soul. I wanted my anthology—if indeed I agreed to undertake such an ambitious task—to explore the most crucial values and meanings that humans have, but I wanted to do that honestly, without sentimentality, facing up to all the suffering and tragedy and random acts of fate that beset us. I agreed to the undertaking when I remembered Augustine's *Confessions*, and indeed used sections of it at the beginning and the very end. But important as Augustine was to my subject and structure, I needed something else, preferably a testimony by a contemporary, and I found it in an essay by Andre Dubus.

I had been following the work of Andre Dubus for some years, for he too was a writer who valued memory and the spiritual quality of ordinary experience; as Tobias Wolff remarks in his fine introduction to Dubus' *Broken Vessels*, a collection of autobiographical essays, Dubus has "an unapologetically sacramental vision of life in which ordinary things participate in the miraculous, the miraculous in ordinary things." In one of the essays in that book, the marvelous "Under the Lights," Dubus gives the account of his childhood experiences as a ball boy for the Lafayette, Louisiana, baseball team in which the crucial event is a home run hit by the most unlikely power hitter on the roster: "We never saw the ball start its descent, its downward arc to earth. For me, it never has. It is rising white over the lights high above the right field fence, a bright and vanishing sphere of human possibility soaring into the darkness beyond our vision." As is true of nearly all essays affirming the value of memory, this essay was written in retrospect, decades after the event; but the essay that comes at the end of the collection is a rare example of a memory not yet given the grace of time's passage; rather, it shows memory at work on tragic concerns of the present and the immediate past—at work, that is, when the help it can bring is almost indistinguishable from anguish, when "human possibility" would seem the remotest of hopes.

That essay, which gives the collection its title, was written at various intervals during Dubus' physical as well as spiritual struggle to recuperate from the accident which left him a cripple, dependent upon a wheelchair for the rest of his life, led to the dissolution of his marriage and cost him the loss of the major custody of his children. Its details are too well known for me to recount them here. The essay is written as if the accident, and all that followed from it, exists in a continuum, and its composition is an obvious attempt to resist the impulse to die. At the close of the essay, that wish for death has been overcome for some months—by those who have helped him (friends, therapists, doctors, his children), by faith in God (despite, Dubus says in an address to the latter, the "sometimes incomprehensible, sometimes seemingly lethal way that You give"), by a human truth confirmed in literature, and by responses he first gained during his Marine Corps training.

Despite its length (it is far and away the longest essay I chose), I included "Broken Vessels" in my anthology, which was published in 1996 under the title of *The Anatomy of Memory*. Dubus' contribution is the moral backbone of that anatomy, the stiffening this particular book required—and the stiffening that all of us have need of, if we are to keep hope and human possibility alive within the atmosphere of the imperiled but shining little globe that is our home.

To a Distant Island, **James McConkey's** re-creation of Anton Chekhov's 6,500-mile journey to Sakhalin Island in Siberia, has been reissued by Paul Dry Books.

James Hughes Meredith

Sacrifice, Sacrament, Sandwiches, Family

I never knew Andre Dubus, but I've lately read most of his writings and find his work as distilled and powerful as Hemingway's in his early short stories. I also understand from writers who knew Andre personally that he was most generous and modest about his work. These praises said, I need to say I have struggled mightily in coming to a conclusion about what to think about Dubus as a writer and as a man.

In *Meditations from a Movable Chair*, Dubus' prose is illuminated by the grace he managed to discover after his accident left him physically crippled. Although I still own my legs, I have had my writing hand crushed so badly that I had to learn to write again, I have had jaw surgery so extensive that recovery sent me to a living hell that I almost did not emotionally come back from, and I recently wished to die following a burst appendix from which I was almost not saved. There have been additional injuries, too. I understand all I want to about pain. And I also understand a little about living with that pain. In his essay "Sacraments," we see Dubus work to transform his own pain into giving by constructing sandwiches for his children; an act he asserts is "parallel" with transubstantiation, or at least "moving in the same direction." Dubus writes that

> A sacrament is physical, and within it is God's love; as a sandwich is physical, and nutritious and pleasurable, and within it is love, if someone makes it for you and gives it to you with love; even harried or tired or impatient love, but with love's direction and concern, love's again and again wavering and distorted focus on goodness; then God's love too is in the sandwich.

While I feel there is significant truth in this passage, it also seems difficult for us mortals to fully discern it, much less to assert this "truth," as does Dubus. Only a man who has suffered greatly, who has lost not only legs but things precious to a caring man could see God's power and mercy in such a mundanity as a sandwich, but it is precisely this grace which makes the mature Dubus such a moving and dignified writer. Consider: "If I could give my children my body to eat, again and again without losing it, my body like the loaves and fishes going endlessly into mouths and stomachs, I would do it." Only a man, a person, who lives spiritually in the grace of God could believe that "you can receive and give sacraments with a telephone," a feat which I, separated from my children and other loved ones too, now believe in.

As a Catholic who early divorced—the union was subsequently annulled—and by necessity had to leave, I condole with Dubus' need to tender spiritual love to his children. It sometimes is all that a man can offer and should not be brazenly condemned by those who have not suffered the experience of children living in a separate home. But I do confess that I'm much bothered by Dubus' single-minded devotion to an art form—the short story—that seemingly provided little financial support for his ever-increasing family. There especially seems to have been no opportunity to give much money to his last set of children since he himself was so strapped from his hospitalization and recovery. On the other hand, I do appreciate Dubus' need for perfection in his art, whether it paid him financially well or not. What Dubus' most personal life experiences—three failed marriages, separations from six children in all—provide for is a rare and distilled art of the highest integrity while offering puny commercial value in a culture that little values such things. Although Andre's son—Andre III—is finding both artistic and commercial success today in the novel form, Dubus' children had to have suffered in a world that demands money to even survive. Whether he ever knew it or not, it is as if Dubus also had to sacrifice his children— lambs upon the altar—for his art. Dubus was not alone in his suffering for perfection in his chosen art form, his family sacrificed, too—in fact, on a certain level, was sacrificed. Ultimately, Andre seems to have found transcendent love in sacraments, and found, too, I believe, that at the heart of communion is a discovery of not only self but also community.

Coda: I admit *I* am struggling with Dubus—his life, his art, and his vision. His giving and taking. The complexity of *his* struggle, guiding me through the complexity of mine. Right or wrong, I have always felt that Protestants comfortably think of themselves as a community of the saved while Catholics painfully consider themselves a community of sinners who struggle daily with their salvation. For me, Dubus' writing is a record of men and women who, combating personal demons and the consequences of sin, often find mysterious ways to overcome their adversities. Dubus' work cuts this particular Catholic to the bone, and moves me to recommit my faith in the power of communion and to renew my trust in the love of family and community over self. The tribute I offer to Andre is to say that the struggles and sacrifices he and those near him made for his work is an odd, clear, and confusing mix of deep magnanimity and utter selfishness. But because of this life and this work, I have been moved to profound struggle with both my own demons—such as drinking, smoking, and selfishness—and the better angels of my nature—giving, caring, and the search for family and community. Andre Dubus' work reminds me more of Milton's *Paradise Lost* than the work of other American writers he's often compared to. Although Dubus worked in the short story form, his corpus is epic in its fundamental scope—it is about the very soul of man. His earlier work seems to me to depict men and women lost, living in a "darkness visible," but his later work—*Dancing After Hours* and *Meditations*—seems to me to be about the possibility of salvation, especially through family. I have been touched and am most grateful for it.

Our Father who art in Heaven . . .

James Hughes Meredith has written widely on Ernest Hemingway and F. Scott Fitzgerald, as well as on The American Civil War, WWI, and WWII.

Chris Offutt

Mr. Dubus

I did not hear of Andre Dubus until I was a thirty-year-old M.F.A. student at Iowa. My fellow students were younger and better educated than I was. They talked about Andre Dubus in casual terms, as if he lived around the corner and you could expect to run into him any day. They referred to him as "Andre." He sounded like someone I might get along with. Eventually I knew who Andre Dubus really was, and I went straight to the bookstore. I read a story of his while standing in the aisle, then bought every book of his in stock.

My wife understood that I read authors not books. When I got home, she saw my pile of books and asked who it was. "Andre," I said, and read for several hours. Now, twelve years later, with his influence strong on my own work, I realize that I was wrong. The name of the author was "Mr. Dubus."

Chris Offutt's most recent story collection is *Out of the Woods*.

Robert Olmstead

Our Daughters

The details of my first meeting Andre have drifted into the ether, like the signal of a radio escaped the earth. I don't remember with exactitude, it being a long time ago, but that meeting, it's out there still.

I never have remembered well, and so am grateful to be a writer as it is a calling that favors powerful, selective, and imperfect memory. But I remember it was in Syracuse, New York, where I was a writing student. Andre had come to town to read and afterwards there was a party at Toby Wolff's house. When Andre walked into a room, the air changed. It became electric, ozonic, catalytic. When he held forth, he was loud and robust and his laugh unbridled. He was dignified as only the blue collar can be, which is to say, dignified by constraint and shyness around strangers. Easy to tell he'd like to get from the handshakes to the arm-wrestling as quickly as possible.

When he found out I was from New Hampshire, he declared it to be the most redneck state north of the Mason-Dixon. I could not disagree and suddenly we were kindred. Plus, I had become a father that year, a new baby girl into the world, now eighteen years old and a very fine artist with dreams of becoming a painter and I don't praise her enough, but already she is too shrewd for any old compliment.

He and I talked about the beauty of having daughters. How daughters are born wise. How even as infants, they cut their eyes at you the way grown women do. How they are like a needle in the heart and how easy it would be to die for them. I don't remember much more, but we drank bourbon and the room was suffused with a feeling the color of amber and it was warm and in Toby's living room that night, we all seemed to have the sure knowledge that sustains you until later in life when you realize how fragile your being. We simply didn't know how quickly it would come.

After the party we all went to a joint on Westcott Street. I haven't been back in the longest time, but in those days the street was scene to the lowlife and the midlife, university fringe and forever students, artists, writers, pushers, habitués of guerrilla culture, slummers in the demimonde of life. I trust it hasn't changed much as Syracuse seems to lurch from one failed renewal to another on a wheel that slips its cogs, its glorying last when the Erie Canal opened. I remember that someone of us was pushed and suddenly was the heart-stopping, galvanizing moment before a bar explodes. Even now I can see it and feel it. The hair on my arms and neck as if static charged. We weren't writers, no. We were men before men had two names. We were dogs squared and poised, bodies curved and hackled and sniffing the air without motion and Andre was at the nucleus of this combustible moment. Then it passed and wasn't that the funniest damn thing. We all shook hands and tumbled out the door stinking of beer, smoke, sweat and the burn of adrenalin. By God, we'd have taken them. By the Jesus, we'd have given a good accounting of ourselves and we were thrilled at the prospect, because no matter what happened, we knew we'd be the ones writing the ending. We'd get to tell it, whichever way we wanted.

I would never see him again after that night, but this is what I have discovered with literary friendships: once forged they are never broken. In nature, they are of the military, the fraternity, sisterhood, brotherhood, and can be dissimilar and disparate and unlikely and all without need of maintenance. Even our most dysfunctional families share their unbreakable and incomprehensible bonds. You are in the world and your writer friends are in the world and you know this and unless you learn otherwise, you know that they are doing what you are doing, getting up each morning and having the same sinking feeling as they move from the bed to the desk. In fact, I just called Jay McInerney on the phone, after being out of touch for a year and the first thing he said was, Bob, I was just thinking about you. From anyone else, I might have thought it a pleasantry, but not from him. That night on Westcott Street, Jay was there too.

Then there was the accident and I could not believe it. How could a man be hit by a speeding vehicle and live? Well, because it was Andre. It seemed but days from when we'd met. It might be an insensitive observation on my part, but in his literary realm of existence, Andre would have visited such an accident upon one of his own characters. How ironic for a writer who eschewed such cleverness as irony on the page to be struck down this way. But it isn't ironic, because with Andre there is never any irony. There is nothing cold and distant and effete. As a fiction maker, he was never content to arrange the universe such that the circumstances dictate the outcome. With Andre people are transcendent. With Andre, life is always fertile and consequential. People endure and through their endurance they learn, or they do not learn and if they do not learn, well then, they learn that. The blood is never separated from the bone and is always close to the skin. Living always comes with the cost of living. In Andre's work, there is always a God, but he is Andre's God and maybe that's why the other God allowed such a deeply regrettable occurrence.

Then, years later, I met Annie Williams and she introduced me to her father Tom. I am ashamed to say that Tom is a disappearing writer and that is a curse on all of us who are responsible for sustaining and transmitting the glory of literature. I fear we have conceded too much of the public ground to the politicians, privateers, vaudevillians and nincompoop citizens among us who merely inhale and exhale and suddenly become famous because, for instance, they live next door to a murderer. Do presidents still invite writers to the White House? Did they ever?

When I met Tom Williams he was at the end of his life. He was dying of cancer, but Annie introduced us and I became a friend of his in the short time he had left. He'd read a book of mine and said that he liked it and that meant the world to me. It would be one of the last books he'd read, if not the last, and also we talked about Andre. I told Tom how Andre said New Hampshire was the most redneck state north of the Mason-Dixon and Tom grinned and agreed. His voice was ragged and he was not patient in needing to speak. He fought to speak and his words came in ordered declarations as would be expected from a great mind inside a swiftly failing vessel. He told me that he had talked to Andre recently and told him he had to have that goddamn leg cut off. I asked him what he meant and he explained to me, as if I were a bit of the dimwit, that Andre should have the goddamn leg cut off because it was no good. It was always getting infected and it would never be anything useful and if he had the leg cut off he could get some new legs and he could learn to walk again.

What could I say? I thought how only a man dying of a cancer in his brain could tell another man to cut off his last leg, however feeble that leg might be. I have since thought how rational that advice and have often wondered if I could give such advice, or receive such advice and if the time should come, I still don't know what I'd do.

Then Andre died. When I heard the news he died, I was walking into class and a student told me. He'd heard the news on the radio that afternoon. He then asked me if I knew Andre's work, but the life had gone out of me and I could not speak and to write these words is to have him die all over again, him and Tom Williams and a part of me too.

We are not used to writers dying. Even the dead ones don't really seem dead. They live on our shelves and in our minds and they speak to us every day. Even in death they are insistent and eloquent, moving and beguiling and we commune with them. It is not their death we must survive, but their dying.

My daughter knows Andre, though she never met him. She knows him because I knew him and she knows him because she reads him on the page. This knowing she triangulates with her own life to draw the map of who she is. Balzac said that few novelists are so cruel as to bear children. I would suggest that if they do, for their own good, they should have daughters.

Robert Olmstead's most recent book is the memoir *Stay Here With Me*.

Tim Parrish

Gift

The best writers give gifts. I only met Andre Dubus once, but he was one of those writers.

When I was 20, I entered a fiction contest named after Andre's mother and judged by Andre and his sister, Beth Michel (her name at that time). The story I submitted was loosely based on the stabbing of a friend's future brother-in-law in the brother-in-law's front yard and the ensuing complications when my friend wanted to enlist me in the burning of a house as revenge (I declined). To my amazement, my story was voted a finalist, and Beth took me on as a pupil and introduced me to Andre's work.

Even though I had grown up and still lived in Louisiana, I had never heard of Andre, but the stories in *Adultery and Other Choices* resonated powerfully and familiarly with me as soon as I read them. Right off the bat, Andre mentioned Baton Rouge, my place, something I had never before seen in a published story. More importantly, in his narratives about Paul Clement, Andre dealt with subject matter I understood, a boy, and then a man, struggling to please a withholding father. In all the stories of the collection, Andre was investigating the trials of finding one's place in the larger society of men, but the intersections of one story, "Cadence," with my life were remarkable: Like Paul Clement, I'd grown up in a macho culture, a culture that persuaded my brother to volunteer for Vietnam, a culture that kept me playing organized sports long after I'd encountered enough coaches with knacks for abuse but none for teaching to have sent a clearer head to more useful pursuits. My summer job between high school and college was as a laborer on a chemical plant construction site, the only white kid on a crew of men breaking hard dirt as the south Louisiana sun assaulted us from seven to three-thirty every day. When I came home from work the first night and collapsed, complaining about my soggy, aching arms, my father, a former Mississippi sharecropper, stood over me and told me I had to learn how to work if I was going to be a man. Although later I would see other aspects of "Cadence," the story originally seemed to me a document revealing the idiocy of trying to please angry, limited men, even at the cost of betraying a friend. More significantly, the writing was the most muscular, knowing and authoritative I had ever encountered. I wanted to write like that to tell my own stories about a violent urban Louisiana.

Several years passed. I graduated from college, got married and divorced, went a little crazy, started singing in a band called The Human Rayz, and, of course, became a high school teacher. Then Beth told me that Andre was coming to town to read and asked if I would like to be his driver. I gladly volunteered. It was February 1986, just months before Andre's accident. I was no longer the newly encouraged finalist in a regional contest, but rather a person who hadn't written in two years and felt the lack. I needed something, maybe a swift kick, and I was hoping meeting Andre would provide it.

Andre beamed with ruddy good cheer and bravado when I picked him up at the Baton Rouge airport, and we swapped stories and told jokes all the way back to his sister's. She lived on a somewhat busy, although dimly lit street, and after I'd parked on the shoulder, Andre stepped to the rear of my car, stripped out of the jeans he'd worn on the plane, slipped on a pair of slacks and stuck a sheathed buck knife into his boots. I appreciated the performance.

The next day, Andre graced my AP IV English class with a powerful reading of "A Father's Story" (haunting foreshadowing considering the accident in the story). I had never encountered a story of such deep meditation and spiritual declaration, a story of such complication and flawed honesty. Even my students, who seemed a little bored by the older narrator's ruminations early in the story, became entranced and then transported by the drama of the daughter's hit-and-run and by the conflict of a father protecting his daughter at the risk of his own soul. By the end of the reading, I was burning to write again.

That night, Don Hendrie, the director of Alabama's writing program and Andre's friend, drove over from Tuscaloosa and joined us, and as the beer and stories flowed, the two of them convinced me I should apply to Bama's M.F.A. program. I'd told Andre of my difficulties writing since that story he had read for the contest years ago, told him how I'd become so dissatisfied with my own work and overwhelmed with the grind of five class preps and the other responsibilities of a high school teacher that I felt like a hack. He listened and commiserated, although what I was saying was whiny, maybe even pathetic. Then he told me to give him a story to read so that he could write a letter of recommendation, and even though the work I had felt old and clunky, I trusted him enough to do it.

The next day at the airport he signed my copy of *Adultery and Other Choices*, handed it to me and shook my hand. Later, in his letter to Alabama's program, Andre would talk about my story's many flaws and my immaturity as a writer, but he would finish with the recommendation that I should be admitted because I had "that elusive it." Early on in Tuscaloosa I floundered as a writer, and I clung to Andre's words when not much else seemed encouraging. In the worst workshop (which my friends are sick of hearing me tell about), the teacher tossed my manuscript to the center of the table and pronounced it "hyperbolic crap." Even though he was right, I had the same urge to go at him as I had my spitting, cursing, poking high-school basketball coach years before. Still, I listened as he asked if I'd read Andre's story "Cadence." When I nodded, he told me to read it again, even though he didn't offer why.

As I re-read it I saw some of the ridiculousness of boot camp and the need to please a drill sergeant transferred to the workshop, but I knew that couldn't be all of it. So I read the story again and again, the weight of it more and more like a pack and a rifle, my reader's legs growing as weary as my actual legs those basketball afternoons when I'd run hundreds of bleachers in my weighted vest; as weary as my arms when I'd stabbed the ground with my shovel until my arms went—like that young Marine's body humping up that hill—to a rhythm beyond numbness; as weary as my brain when I'd rewritten the same scene time after time after time to try and . . . Ah.

I set the book on my lap and rubbed my eyes. I pictured Andre far away, battling with a confinement that betrayed the athlete's ability and freedom he'd labored so hard to achieve, and thought of that character in "A Father's Story" sorting through the details of each day, through his own spirit, his life changed by a collision with the bumper of a car. Then I thumbed back to the front of my book where Andre's handwriting looped and flowed: "For Tim, with thanks for the friendship in Baton Rouge, and wishes for resilience in all." And I understood.

Tim Parrish's most recent story collection is *Red Stick Men*.

Richard Ravin

Remembering Andre Dubus

My friend Andre liked bad movies and unfiltered cigarettes and baseball and good-looking women. His son, Andre III, put words to it at his funeral, shouting from the pulpit: "My daddy was *big*." Andre had big feelings and big faith and it was his big, generous heart that finally gave out on Feb. 24. His friend Bob found him slumped in his special shower chair, the water running cold. They were planning to watch "Die Hard" on Andre's brand-new stereo TV. "Now we got Sensurroouund," he'd been saying all day.

I always thought Andre's beauty as a writer was his patience with the line, playing out his sentences longer and longer, note after note like a scat solo by one of the singers he collected, Ella Fitzgerald or June Christie or Betty Carter. I don't think he'd been bred to patience; maybe he learned it in his wheelchair, where everything is three times slower and three times more difficult, showering and dressing and binding up the better leg in its brace and propping himself into his seat, pushing himself down the hall.

I got to know him five years ago, when I joined the writing workshop he held in his house on Thursday nights, and I'd come early sometimes and find Andre running late. More than once, he burst out of the bathroom naked and still wet and expected no lag in the conversation while he pulled on his T-shirt and sweat pants, tied a red bandanna around his amputated knee. Then he tilted partway out of his chair, farted and sighed a schoolboy's delight at the release. He loved having a body, even the damaged one that survived being hit by a car.

This wasn't easy to watch, to see how scarred Andre was or how strong the part was that wasn't scarred, but Andre was transparent to his friends. He called himself a cripple and the rest of us bipeds, picking the words with a writer's precision and fuck the politics of empowerment. His pain was part of the truth of how he lived, nothing to be embarrassed by.

You could guess when he'd had to stack up on his medication, watch him tongue down his end-of-day Halcyon. He talked easily about his confusions and fears and furies, and to be in the presence of one of his rants could leave you panting. If you've read his stories and essays, you know he had a special concern for the poor and the forgotten, and when the president passed his vicious welfare revamp in 1996, Andre swore Clinton was the last fucking Democrat he'd ever vote for, no better than a Republican.

His characters were the wounded and the weak and the stubborn: Louise in "The Fat Girl" and Luke in "A Father's Story" and Matt in "Killings." Sinners all, like Andre—there were three ex-wives, don't forget—characters hammered out on the page, every one of them demanding our compassion and respect. A character's flaws never need defending or explaining, Andre said. They're just human, that's all.

Andre began the writing workshop after the accident that cost him his legs, and it ran for 12 years until a week before he died. He never charged a fee, even when he was hard up for cash. He felt companionable with writers, loved hearing our complaints and shared his own, loved hearing about our successes as though something good had happened in the family. Putting money to that would ruin the music.

For all his outrageousness, he was a gentle cheering section at our center, scrawling our pages with a modest check mark or "Wow!" and telling us, almost by incantation, that what our stories needed was an envelope and a stamp and someone to send us a check. He tied himself in knots to find something to praise in even the least deserving work, lost sleep if he thought he'd been too harsh.

I forgot how famous he was, forgot the wall of translations in German and Dutch and Japanese, forgot the MacArthur Genius Award and the Rea Award and the short list for the National Book Critics, forgot the messages on his answering machine from Tobias Wolff or postcards from Kurt Vonnegut or Anne Beattie. Andre treated us as equals, and when it was his turn to read—he brought to the workshop every essay and story that went into his last two books—Andre's hands were just as shaky as the rest of ours; he was so anxious one of the last times out, he convinced a woman in the group to do the reading in his place.

The story was a period western with a black cowboy hero and a rape victim and more than one killing. It was sentimental and strong and filled with the powerful sense of place that hallmarked Andre's work. There was a debate, though, of the sort we often had at Andre's house over some practical issues in the material. The main character digs a grave and builds a coffin and buries a man over the course of an afternoon, and many of us felt there wasn't enough time to accomplish all that labor. Maybe he was tired that day, but Andre let the criticism run by him; the business required the length of an afternoon, he could picture in his mind how it would go.

Later, Andre's two sons took up the same argument, and their old man challenged them to build his coffin when the time came and see what was true and what wasn't. It took Jeb and Andre III more than 15 hours, the two of them, with power tools. Andre would have hated that. He loved getting the details exactly right. As he always told us, that's what a writer does.

Richard Ravin is a film, television, and Web producer who lives in Massachusetts. He is currently completing his first novel.

Darrell Spencer

Let's Say We Disagreed about Baseball

I'm coming in the side door here. Or is it the bathroom window?

I'm unsure of my homage. I never met Andre Dubus. Can't add to the legend, the myth, the canon of anecdotes. I don't know the man's hat size. Have heard no gossip, and I am not privy to the scuttlebutt.

I see photos, and I think: Big-hearted. Robust. Savvy. Wily. I sense he would have bridled at my using such cartoon words, as if I were turning him into a blurb. I don't think Andre Dubus was a man I would have run with. We were not, as they say, of the same tribe. He hunted. He fished. I golf. Did he? He was a BoSox fan. In "Brothers," he says, "For me, baseball is more real than much of what I do." For me, football—yes. Basketball—yes. But baseball—no. What did the Phillies' John Kruk say to the lady fan who chastised him for smoking? I'm not an athlete, lady; I'm a baseball player.

Dubus listened to Sinatra. There you go. We could have opened the conversation there. I'd tell him about my pal's dad comping me tickets to see Dino and Frank and Sammy Davis, Jr. I'd tell him about growing up in Las Vegas. I believe he would have listened hard.

Smart. There's another word. It is clear from the writing that he was smart about people, that he honored his own desiderata: "[A]t the desk a writer must try to be free of prejudice, meanness of spirit, pettiness, and hatred; strive to be a better human being than the writer normally is, and to do this through concentration on a single word, and then another, and another." I read Dubus' fiction, his essays, and I think: Big-hearted. Robust. Savvy. Wily. He cut through the shit; he is the one who, after all the sadness is inhaled and all the speculation has failed, understands why a pilot died: "the pilot was killed because he flew airplanes from a ship at sea." Dubus loved pistols but he gave them up. He loved to run, but he had to give that up. Still he seems to have been a demon in that wheelchair. I bet he was not a man who was at peace except for a minute here and there, say, when Liv Ullmann rested her hand on his shoulder. He has just "told her everything," about the accident, about loss and fear and about his dreams of walking. He tells us that she said to him, "You can't compensate."

His reply?

"No," I said. "I cannot compensate."

The heart skips a beat.

He adds: "Then my breast filled with peace."

But for how long? A fortnight, he claims.

Two pals of mine met Dubus, one, Rob Roberge, when Rob was a student. How'd he strike you? I wanted to know. Protective, Rob said. Dubus had spent a great deal of class time talking about teaching his boys to box. Religious, Rob said. Religion worries Rob, particularly in a writer.

You see the religion in Dubus' essays and in the stories. Weekday Mass ("I believe most Catholics go to mass for the same reason I do: to take part in ritual, and to eat the body of Christ"). The Eucharist ("I go to Mass because the Eucharist is there"). Priests. Take the often anthologized "A Father's Story"—Luke Ripley (the storyteller), and the priest buddy, and the fierce and unnerving love the story depicts: at what cost betrayal? Betrayal of the community. Betrayal of thy neighbor. All in the name of love and without hesitation, unless the telling of the story is itself a hesitation, and I don't believe it is. No, the story *is* fierce, but it is also gentle. There is a holy silence in the unsettling conclusion, Luke Ripley's calling God on the carpet when God tells him that he—that Luke Ripley—loves "in weakness," and Luke replies, "As You love me."

That's not your father's old-time religion.

It is not, I don't think, the kind of religion in a writer that worries my friend. Luke Ripley tells God he loves his daughter more than he loves truth. Isn't that what fiction is all about? Screw truth—that big-winged hairy abstraction. Flannery O'Connor's neighbor announces this fact when she returns the stories she's borrowed from O'Connor, stories O'Connor herself wrote: "Well, them stories just gone and shown you how some folks *would* do." To which O'Connor adds: "[W]hen you write stories, you have to be content to start exactly there—showing how some specific folks *will* do, *will* do in spite of everything."

Dubus offers a prayer to John Kennedy, asks Jack to help him write a story. You got to like a guy who would do that.

I told Rob the Dubus I see in photographs looks like a man who would have played linebacker in the '50s for the Chicago Bears.

"When they wore leather helmets," Rob said.

We agreed.

Another pal, Bruce Jorgensen, driving from Cambridge to Plymouth, NH, realized that he was passing near to where Dubus lived at the time, and he dropped by. Bruce didn't know the man. Had been put on to Dubus by Fred Busch. Dubus is good, Busch said to Bruce, just as, years later, on a sunny afternoon in Utah, Bruce would say to me, Dubus is good. So it goes—writer to writer to writer. The gifts. Read so-and-so. You do, and you'll learn something about writing. Bruce got directions from the receptionist at Bradford College where Dubus was teaching. He rang the bell, feeling like an interloper. He had no idea what he was going to say, but came up with the password: I'm a reader, he said to the woman who answered the door, and she—Dubus' wife, Peggy Rambach—welcomed him in. As did Dubus, who happened, right at the minute, to be in the shower. Come in. Wait. Bruce spent the evening. "Such wonderful company," my pal tells me.

Like I said, Big-hearted and so on.

Let's say we did disagree about baseball. My sense is he would have discussed the question seriously and with wit.

Dubus held forth for my pal. He regaled him with stories. He kept calling for Foster Lager. He mimicked Bill Cosby. "Got him right on," Bruce says.

Well, Bruce needs to tell that story in his own words.

Me, what I know is the writing. Dubus is good, Busch said. The day Bruce passed along that message I bought *Adultery and Other Choices* and spent the afternoon and evening reading. I came late to writing fiction, felt like a greenhorn learning from writers my own age, the already established. Francois Camoin, Amy Hempel, Grace Paley, Lee K. Abbott, Joy Williams, Stanley Elkin, Barry Hannah, William Gass. I liked bumpy prose. The jingle-jangled. Hopped up sentences that skipped a beat but held on. That flew by the seat of their pants.

Dubus was writing sentences like 10-penny nails.

From "Adultery":

> The apartment is small, half of the first floor of a small two-story house, and it is the place of a man who since his boyhood has not lived with a woman except housekeepers in rectories. The front room where they are standing, holding each other lightly now like dancers, is functional and, in a masculine disorderly way, orderly; it is also dirty.

Exacting. Clear. Rigorous. Big-hearted.

What I learned from Dubus was generosity and trajectory. His work was utterly alien to me—his indefatigable sentences: the simplicity of their declarations.

What did I want from Dubus?

To be taught to do other than what I was doing. To learn choices. I studied how he built stories. Above all what I sensed here was a writer who could teach me to do what I most wanted to do: tell you a story in a straightforward way and break your heart while I was at it. Amy Hempel tells us that Gordon Lish tells us that we as readers must feel "the pressure of the heart enlarging." She quotes Lish: "The writer must persuade you that if you don't listen he'll die, and if you listen he'll save your life, and if you *don't* listen you'll die a lot harder—there's the exchange."

No one's going to save your life. Who's kidding who? Nothing holds up at 3 a.m. But a few writers can fool you into thinking they've solved being alive. What they offer is: hang on. There's the real exchange—the voice that is so convincing you'll not forgive it for what it has to say to you.

I see the photos of Dubus, and I don't see a man at peace, not before or after the accident. There is something different about the essays in *Meditations from a Movable Chair*, from which I've been quoting. In "Witness" he declares, as he approaches his subject, that he is going to go there and "find the music for it." In the end, he writes: "and I did not find the music. Everything I have written here seems flat: the horns dissonant, the drums lagging, the piano choppy. Today the light came: *I'm here*."

These are the last words in *Meditations*.

Dubus ran. I run. A month ago, visiting California, escaping the sub-freezing temperatures of Ohio, I ran along Venus Beach, and Dubus was on my mind.

Darrell Spencer's most recent collection, *CAUTION Men in Trees*, won the 2000 Flannery O'Connor Award for Short Fiction.

Philip G. Spitzer

"I am a short-story writer"

Nearly thirty years ago I received the manuscript of a collection of short stories by Andre Dubus. I had been recommended to him by an editor I knew only by name. I never did find out why she recommended me, in particular. I saw from the cover letter that Mr. Dubus had, earlier, published a novel at the Dial Press. And all of the short stories in the collection had appeared in impressive literary magazines. *I knew of course that even if this collection of stories turned out to be one that deserved to be published, publishers would respond in the following manner: This is a worthy short-story collection, and we would be interested in publishing it if we can publish a novel by the author first.*

When I read the manuscript, *Separate Flights,* I considered it the best work of fiction I had read in many years. I called Mr. Dubus and told him how the stories had moved me and how I would consider it a privilege to represent him and this collection. However, I advised him that publishers would likely admire the manuscript, as well, but that they would say, *This is a worthy short story collection, and we would be interested in publishing it if we can publish a novel by the author first.*

"But," Mr. Dubus insisted, "I'm a short-story writer." I asked if he ever considered writing another novel at some point, should a publisher ask. "I am a short-story writer," he replied. I asked if he ever wrote a short story or a novella that, perhaps, got away from him and threatened to become a longer piece. I don't recall his reply. But a few years later, following a similar conversation, he sent me the short story "Waiting," one of my favorite stories. It was, I think, eleven manuscript pages long. Andre told me it had been 78 pages in first draft. I never asked him about a novel again.

By the end of that initial phone conversation, we agreed that we belonged together. We were about to accompany each other on a quixotic journey in probably the most unlikely and unprofessional author-agent relationships possible. Later on, when we got to know each other, we realized that our decision to work together tantamount to exchanging a vow of poverty.

When the first editor responded to the manuscript of *Separate Flights,* I called Mr. Dubus to tell him how much the editor had shared my admiration for his book. I told him that the editor would be interested in publishing the story collection if they could publish a novel by him first. He asked me how long this would continue. I assured him that he had written an extraordinary book of fiction and that it would certainly be published. He asked when. I told him I didn't know in which decade but that I would do everything I could. It turned out to be only years, instead of decades.

We would have similar conversations until, finally, Andre stopped asking what publishers were saying about his book. He would call asking if there was any progress. I would say no, and Andre would tell me how the Red Sox were doing. We had by then met in person and had become close friends. We shared our love of baseball, our children, and our vices. We shared our experiences as husbands and fathers, our failures and occasional successes. (I want to say that we bonded, but that always sounds too close to "bondage.") Our friendship deepened far beyond our professional association.

Finally, one day, a publisher from Boston, David Godine, accepted *Separate Flights* for publication. The advance was small, but a quality house would publish the book. David was enthusiastic about Andre's work, and when *Separate Flights* was published, it received extraordinary reviews. Predictably, New York publishers called to say how pleased they would be to publish Mr. Dubus' next book of stories. There was no more talk of a novel. Andre was having financial difficulties. The publishers in question offered five times the advance that David Godine was able to offer. Andre's response was simple: Where were these people when Godine took a chance on me? David Godine would publish Andre for the next twenty years. We never even discussed an alternative during those years. This only confirmed to me that Andre was a man of principle with the courage to stand by his convictions. To this day, if ever I am faced with a dilemma of a moral or ethical nature, I ask myself, what would Andre want me to do. I listen to his voice and pray, in my secular way, that I might be half the man that my friend Andre was.

Alfred Knopf published Andre's last two books. This was after the accident that had left Andre in a wheelchair and faced with medical bills and other expenses. There was the opportunity to sign a significant contract with Knopf, an opportunity that had not been sought by Andre. The decision to sign was made only after consulting with David Godine and with the assurance, by me, that the publicity generated by Knopf's publication would escalate the sales of the books David had published, which turned out to be the case.

Andre's life and his courage have been well documented. I don't have to relate, here, the stories you have read or heard over the years. Our friendship continued to grow. We spoke on the phone at least once a day, every day except Sunday. Andre would call to ask about my family or to tell me how his kids were doing. Sometimes it was just to tell me about the Red Sox or about a film he had seen, a book he had read or a joke he had heard.

But there was still another side to Andre that I came to love and respect. We did of course talk about writing. This was the passion for him that it is for any great writer. I learned a lot from him about the art and the craft of writing. In 1984 I had the occasion to spend one night a week at Andre's house on the campus of Bradford College. I slept on a cot in his library and would make a point of picking off his shelves and reading books by authors he admired and spoke with. You see, in most of our conversations about writers and writings, the subject was never Andre's own writing but that of other writers. He often seemed to care about other writers more than he cared about himself or his own success.

He often spoke of Gina Berriault and how this fine writer had never received the recognition she deserved. When Andre's last book of short stories *Dancing After Hours* was nominated for a National Book Critics Circle Award, Ms. Berriault's *Women in Their Beds* was nominated too. Andre came to New York, and in the hours prior to the awards ceremony, all he could talk about was how he hoped Gina Berriault would win the National Book Critics Award for fiction. But what about you, Andre? I asked. He said that he had already received enough attention and that no one deserved this award more than Gina. When Ms. Berriault was announced the winner, Andre struggled in his wheelchair to intercept her before she took the stage. He reached for her, giving her his patented hug, congratulating her and telling her how happy he was for her.

Later when the ceremony was over, Andre, the people from Knopf, and others of us went to dinner in a restaurant nearby. All of us except for Andre were mourning the fact that he had not won the NBCC award—until we all saw the joy on Andre's face. Suddenly everyone realized what was happening and the mood of the evening changed dramatically. I had never witnessed anything quite like Andre's reaction, and I am sure I never will again.

Gina Berriault died the same year as Andre. The year-end issue of *The New York Times Magazine* was devoted to portraits of notable people who had died that year. It included a two-page spread about two exceptional and under-appreciated writers, Andre Dubus and Gina Berriault. To me, these portraits live as a testimony to Andre and everything he stood for.

Andre's legacy lives on, however. Months after his death, *House of Sand and Fog*, a novel written by Andre Dubus III was named a Finalist for the National Book Award. Young Andre called to tell me the news. He said that his novel was a finalist and promptly asked, "Do you think that will help sell my dad's books?"

Philip G. Spitzer, Andre Dubus' longtime literary agent, lives in East Hampton, New York.

Lara JK Wilson

Thursday Nighters

On Thursday nights we'd arrive late, unless we were new, in which case we'd be early or on time, and he'd welcome us like old friends and offer spring water or his leftover shrimp étouffée or bread a friend had made for him. He'd greet you from his chair and you'd bend to shake his hand or to hug him, but when you looked at him you'd feel like you were looking up because in your heart, and your mind, you were. If you bothered to check his face for pain, you could barely discern what must have been there; he knew how to conceal it in folds of wit and anecdote. With effort, he'd be boisterous rather than distressed. Without effort, he'd make you feel special, his best friend, someone going somewhere, while he remained humble, as if fame had never been a consideration.

You'd greet everyone and ask about their novel, their story, their essay, their family, vacation, work that paid bills. They, like you, were there to read or to listen and to talk about writing, one another's and that of strangers, good or bad. There, anyone might lament about working hours to get one decent sentence and a few pages of crap. Harsh judgment did not exist. Compassion did, and that made it a rare place, one that was occasionally misunderstood and thus abandoned by those who came for the wrong reasons. For some it was a place to be vulnerable or to receive vindication of some kind, or to feel that being vulnerable was justifiable, maybe even appropriate, and that it was unnecessary to want to be vindicated. We would cheer someone's recently accepted story or a former member's book now published, and if a twinge of envy or frustration threatened to knot our conscience, ultimately, we were grateful to be part of the pulsating scheme of the lives of writers.

We would walk the ramp to the living room. We'd crowd onto the soft dark green sofas, avoiding the long windowseat with mismatched pillows. He would roll toward us and turn on the standing lamp beside his chair. Someone would have brought doughnut holes, or cookies usually from a box but occasionally homemade, and we'd sit in our rect-angle and chatter until one or two people insisted we begin so we could finish before midnight. One writer read. Everyone listened. At the end, he might react with an immediate, YES!, or he might reach into his leather bag for a Nat Sherman and light it and stretch his body back against his chair and hear everyone before he spoke. We did not gut the work, sever its flesh—we praised it, prodded it, probed it, tenderized it with the author to find the knot, the cell of concern. When he finally spoke, he did so, unfailingly, with kindness. He'd quote Chekhov, Hemingway, Dick Yates, Iris Murdoch, Tobias Wolff, and would lighten things up with his whole-soul laugh, cursing and insisting that it is the writer who has the answers. He would agree with the rest of us, or not. He would admit he was wrong. He'd say there are no rules. Be true to the characters. To yourself. It is all in there, he'd say, and he'd circle the air above the manuscript with his finger. Or in here, and he'd touch his head and gesture toward the author. We'd absorb his good grace and his respect for the written word, and his wisdom would waft between us like the presence of a mother tucking in her children after prayers, knowing precisely what to say and whether to leave the light on. And we would drive home an hour or two, for some even three, thinking about what was read, what was said. About language. About images, rhythm, time. And the next day at our desk we would read something and we would write, we could write, we wanted only to write, and we wrote.

And we write.

Lara JK Wilson's short fiction has been published in the *Indiana Review*, *Confronta-tion*, and *American Fiction*. She was awarded a Tennessee Williams Scholarship for the 2001 Sewanee Writers' Conference, where she will continue to work on her first novel.

Robley Wilson

If They Knew Andre

In my first year as editor of *The North American Review*—this would have been 1969—the magazine's fiction editor, Loree Rackstraw, brought in an Andre Dubus short story called "If They Knew Yvonne." It was a gorgeous story; it had to do with adolescence and infatuation and the rigors of being Catholic, and it dealt, ultimately, with betrayal and conscience. I'd never met Andre, though our stays at Iowa were only a year or so apart, and I hadn't then read his novel *The Lieutenant*, but Loree and I both knew a fine story when we saw one. We broke the bank at the NAR, and paid $75 for it.

Not long after the story's appearance, a letter arrived from the office of the Iowa attorney general. It had come to the attention of that state officer that the NAR had published a work lacking in "redeeming social importance"—a short story entitled "If They Knew Yvonne." The offending work had been brought to the attorney general by a member of the Iowa state legislature. The letter included a photocopy of the story, with marginal glosses; I particularly remember the notation *"concupiscence—sexual desire"* and I wondered if the legislator had sent some staff underling to look the word up. The attorney general urged the NAR to "reconsider its standards" for the material we chose to publish.

There was some furor in the Iowa press. We were, after all, a magazine owned by a state university, and that meant we were spending taxpayer money. Vice presidents and deans were convened; responses were weighed. In the end I wrote the attorney general that we felt the magazine's standards were defensible literary ones, but that I was willing to discuss the matter with him whenever and wherever he wished. He didn't respond, and when "If They Knew Yvonne" was selected for that year's *The Best American Short Stories*, you can imagine how pleased we were—and how happily we publicized the honor.

It was a few years later that I met Andre at Bradford College, where he was teaching and I was reading. After the reading we dined at a blue-collar sort of restaurant in Haverhill, then adjourned to Andre's apartment, where he and I, and Peggy Rambach, whom he later married, drank too much wine and sang old songs to the accompaniment of Peggy's guitar. The three of us wrote a song of our own, called "Tequila Eyes"—a collaboration whose words and music are long since lost to a deprived posterity.

Our paths didn't cross often, but the NAR published a number of Andre's stories over the years. I recall "Separate Flights," the title story of one of his collections, and "Contrition," and a sports story called "The Pitcher." There might have been others, but memory has effaced them. What I do especially remember is a story we didn't get to publish. I heard Andre read "A Father's Story" one summer at Indiana University. The story appeared in *Black Warrior Review* while Andre was visiting writer in Tuscaloosa, and it is a nearly perfect exemplar of his work: the war between two kinds of conscience, two kinds of obligation, two loyalties—the one secular, the other religious.

That might have been the last summer before the good deed that cost Andre his leg. I remember meeting him outside the Memorial Union, the morning after his reading. Why hadn't he submitted "A Father's Story" to *The North American Review*, I wondered. He had just come back from his regular morning run, so he was sweaty and healthy and endorphined; we stood in the circular drive of the Union while he caught his breath and explained that after the many stories of his we'd published he felt we'd probably had about enough of him. Never, I said. *Never.*

Conscience. It was Andre's center, in literature, in life. And it must have been as difficult for him as it was for his fictional characters, this balance of loyalty to self against loyalty to something higher than self. I know a number of writers who find *The New Yorker*'s editorial nit-picking annoying, but Andre is the only writer I've heard of—and not from him—who bought back one of his stories, rather than accept an editorial change he disagreed with.

That kind of loyalty, unusual in today's America, brings me back to *The Lieutenant*. It was Andre's first book, published in 1967, and it is his only novel (not counting *Voices from the Moon*, which purports to be a novel but is really a longish short story). When I was invited by *Harper's* to do a retrospective review of *The Lieutenant* on the 20th anniversary of its publication, I concluded:

[Over these years], Andre Dubus has become a masterful short-story writer, an expert explorer of the realms of sacred and profane love set usually in a Catholic moral context, so it is not surprising that from the outset we are asked to view Dan Tierney, the Marine lieutenant protagonist of this book, in terms of "honor," "pride," "loyalty," "esprit," and [with attention to] the nature and responsibility of command. Amid all these old-fashioned abstractions, the novel turns on the question of how masculinity is to be defined, and whether the fact of mercy tempers that definition or only contradicts it.

It seems odd now to remember Andre being accused of writing that lacked redeeming importance of any sort. He may have been no saint, but he knew as much about redemption as anyone who ever held a pen.

Robley Wilson's latest story collection is *The Book of Lost Fathers.*

Nancy Zafris

"Is this really Andre Dubus?"

December 1985. The holiday party for our documentation group had been held at one of the employee's houses. Everybody had gone home early from there. I returned to work, at Digital Computer Company in New Hampshire. It was around 4:00 or 4:30 p.m.; all the cubicles around me were empty, and the vast and high-ceilinged room hummed with its deserted Friday sounds. I liked the place empty. I did my best work alone. That afternoon I couldn't return to the short story I was working on; I was rushing to finish a software guide before I flew to Ohio to spend Christmas with my family.

My phone rang, loud in the silence. "Hey, Nancy Zafris!" a voice called out on the other end. "What are you doing at goddam work!" I figured it was somebody I knew, not from the *goddam*, but more from the correct pronunciation of my last name.

"Hi," I said.

It was Andre Dubus.

Fortunately he kept talking. I had time to let the shock settle in.

After four years of sending out stories, my first one had finally been accepted and published by *Black Warrior Review*. A few weeks earlier I had been notified that Andre Dubus had selected my story as the winner of their annual literary award.

Ironically, Andre Dubus had been why I'd sent to *BWR* in the first place: I had been extremely moved by his wonderful "A Father's Story" in their magazine. I knew he lived in Haverhill, Massachusetts, a stone's throw from my husband's hometown of Newburyport, a seaport village where many Dubus stories were set. Every time we drove down to Newburyport I thought of Andre Dubus, a famous writer doing what he was doing, but not, I imagined, feeling alone and isolated like me. I had not gone to an M.F.A. program, had taken no creative writing classes, and knew no published writers. Each day for four years I had thought several times a day about my mail, wondering if an acceptance letter would finally await me. I'd had some close calls and requests for revisions. Months would go by, me on the edge of my seat. Then a rejection slip.

"You must be Catholic," Andre Dubus boomed into the phone.

"Is this really Andre Dubus?" I asked.

"What the hell are you doing at goddam work?" he said.

He had called my house, got my work number from my husband and bothered to make the second call. He told me he was throwing a Christmas party and he asked me to come. I hung up the phone, stunned. I had one of those moments when you think: *My life has changed.*

I immediately rearranged my travel plans (it was the days of $29 *People Express* flights) so I could attend Andre's party before flying home. "And bring your husband!" Andre had yelled out. "He sounds like a nice guy!" When Andre met my husband Jim, good-looking and wearing khakis and a button-down shirt, he was prepared to treat him like one of the yuppie interlopers changing the face of Newburyport, until he realized Jim was fourth generation, a real *joppa* native. First test passed. Then Andre pulled me around the room, introducing me as a GREAT WRITER!!—in fact (due to Andre, I suspect) several people had read my story and talked to me as if I had won the Pulitzer.

The evening was like a dream, and then Andre, raucous and joking and loud throughout, walked us out to our car, into the clean but bitter cold of the night, and talked quietly for the first time all evening. He said, "I'm 50 years old." He turned to Jim. He had liked hearing the stories Jim told him about Newburyport. He had laughed uproariously when Jim recounted his grandmother calling out to President Taft as he inspected the clam flats, *Hey Bill, how's your bean?*

"My father died when he was fifty," Andre told Jim. "I'm worried about dying. There's so many good books for me still to read." Andre hugged me and wished me Merry Christmas and yelled to me as we left, "I know you're a goddam Catholic!"

When Andre and I became friends, I learned that he did indeed write with a feeling of isolation and aloneness, even before his terrible accident. That was just one of the lessons I learned from him.

Andre's good deed toward me multiplied. His act of kindness had important consequences. He chose me for an anthology he was editing. Through him I met Susan Dodd, who introduced me to her agent. I was a writer writing alone, feeling cut off, and Andre had reached out to me. How many of us, as more established writers, writers at least with some contacts, take the time to bestow attention on a struggling writer—not someone paying to be in our classes, not someone getting a degree, not someone networking—just a writer writing alone, out there somewhere, unconnected, a writer who needs a kind word or a democratic acceptance as a comrade in a hard business? Andre taught me that a simple act is not so simple in its ramifications.

A phone call—such an easy thing. Like his stories, Andre's act of kindness was simple and heartfelt and extraordinary. Like Andre himself.

Nancy Zafris' story collection *The People I Know* won the 1990 Flannery O'Conner Award for Short Fiction.

Critical Studies

She had brown eyes and, ~~lately~~ ~~totally~~

(better word? because of "worn"? drum i)

had lately, in the evening, worn her hair in

a French ~~hair~~ braid; she liked ~~camiller~~ at

stove

36 times →
while hearing
hope

dinner, and after her bath in late afternoon she
~~Her face was tan and pink, her brow and cheeks creased, and
lines moved outward from~~
wore a dress or skirt. ¶ Every morning after

her
eyes
and
lips
when
she
smiled

lines in
future
to her
left

breakfast she walked two miles east to a

red country store, she did this in all weather

except blizzards and ^{you} lightning storms. At the

store she bought ~~the~~ the New York Times and

a package of British cigarettes and sat at

the counter to drink coffee and read. Then she

walked home for lunch, and came in the

front door each day as precisely as a clock

striking noon. She had not done this since the

~~smallest~~ sunlit morning January ~~many~~ when

I yelled?
to face

Robert's ~~busning~~ man broke her legs.
her brow and cheeks creased,

was tan and pink, ~~and~~ lines moved outward from

"The Colonel's Wife"
2nd draft
[signature]

Patrick Samway, S.J.

Andre Dubus: Fictional Truth-Sayer

As I advance in age, I have noticed a serious problem facing today's generation of Roman Catholics: We tend not to unify our discourse, religious, civil or otherwise, into some coherent framework that remains consistent no matter the situation. At home, children learn basic distinctions, involving themselves and others, and the various types of relationships they might or should have in common. In this way, children are taught other generally accepted moral values, though the question is rarely addressed about the significance and application of these values in later life. Too often infantile absolutism remains a lifelong norm.

Curiously, children sense that stories allow them to enter into worlds beyond their ken, where the possible is transmuted into the probable that has, in some fantastic way, a bearing on the lives they lead. Fiction—even when it involves space colonies or talking animals—transfixes them; it is as "real" as any nonfictional events they encounter. Unfortunately—and here is the rub—children are usually not aware that their parents too often speak one language at home (and in church) and another outside the home (or church) that empowers them to act in ways at odds with their language used at home. For adult Roman Catholics, the Christian notion of dying to oneself and to sin in order to rise in glory with the Lord, to cite but one example, becomes too often a private counter-cultural belief that, while retaining its perennial validity, is best disguised or simply not talked about it in public. Thus many Catholics today compartmentalize language and have difficulty synthesizing disparate modes of speech, weakening their ability to make those connections that give coherence to what they say and believe and do.

Yet, at times, our basic juvenile instincts about literature kick in, allowing us to read and see and hear words that depict situations and conflicts that form part of some intelligible whole, even if we do not understand it wholly. Truth (another counter-cultural word) is more than a series of philosophical propositions that need to be tested; in works of literature, for example, truth resides in words and phrases that evoke images that allow us to appreciate once again—because we tend to forget so easily—the depths of the human heart in conflict with itself, as William Faulkner knew so well.

Fiction permits me as an adult to enter an arena / environment / classroom / space where truths about the human situation can appear and be seen with a clarity I too often forget exists. Of all the stories and novellas I have read over the years, those by Andre Dubus consistently manifest the truths of the human heart that most make credible sense, due in large measure, I believe, to the seemingly ordinary characters he has created and the convincing situations they find themselves in—not unsimilar, I am quick to add, to what James Joyce, John Cheever, Eudora Welty, Katharine Anne Porter, Peter Taylor, and Faulkner have also done in *their* own ways. Of all the 20th-century American fiction writers who happen to be Catholic, Dubus, for me at least, leads the group. I had long recognized his literary gifts, even to the point of beginning to compile a master bibliography of his works that was eventually published in the February 1987 issue of the French literary journal *Delta*, before I first met him in the Boston University Book Store in the fall of 1983.

It happened that I had written Dubus nine years before to obtain permission to use one of his stories, "Over the Hill," for a collection of short stories, entitled *Stories of the Modern South*, that Ben Forkner and I were in the process of editing. Though Dubus had been born and raised in southwest Louisiana, educated from third grade to his senior year in high school at the Christian Brothers' Cathedral School in Lafayette, and eventually graduating from McNeese State College in 1958, he had moved by then first to southern New Hampshire and subsequently to Haverhill, Massachusetts, to teach creative writing, beginning in 1966, at the now closed Bradford College. While he brought with him the native intelligence and discerning savvy of a down-home Cajun, honed first by five and a half years as a Marine and then by two and a half years at the University of Iowa's Writers' Workshop, he discovered in and around Haverhill those whom he could transform into the protagonists of his own Yoknapatawpha. After our initial meeting, I occasionally visited Andre (we were soon on a first-name basis) and his wife, Peggy, and Cadence, their young daughter; living and teaching in nearby Chestnut Hill that academic year allowed me to drive easily to Haverhill. Peggy, an open and considerate individual who had grown up in New York City, seemed quite comfortable in her New England surroundings. As a former student of Andre, she too had published fiction, something that Andre encouraged her to do. Then, as now, Cadence (as did Madeleine after she was born in January 1987) radiated life—and Andre totally delighted in both.

Even after I moved to New York City in June 1984, where I became the literary editor of *America*, a weekly journal of opinion, I would continue to see Andre (both before and after his "biped days," as he was wont to say) and gradually came to know the larger Dubus family, particularly the children of Andre and his gracious first wife Patricia (Suzanne, Andre III, John Ethan Burke ["Jeb"], and Nicole), as well as Andre's sisters, both of whom live in Baton Rouge, Louisiana: Kathryn Selleck and the novelist who publishes under her maiden name, Elizabeth Nell Dubus. My friendship with Andre just occurred, though in hindsight there was a basis for it: Andre was a devout Roman Catholic who wrote fiction; I am a Jesuit priest who teaches and writes about (Southern) literature. We often shared views on religion and literature, seeking to locate by all sorts of means of triangulation what they had in common and why they were so essential to both of us.

A burly individual, with powerful hugging arms and a somewhat quiet raspy voice, except when he exploded into laughter, Andre kept most of his life's adventures inside himself, though he revealed in his essays those he thought important enough to share (beginning with his early love of the Class C baseball team, the Lafayette Brahman Bulls, which he later transferred to the Boston Red Sox). I have seen Andre in several periods of great pain and suffering, including the few days I spent with him in Massachusetts General Hospital after his July 23, 1986 accident on I-93 north of Boston, to know that he rooted his life in that of Jesus the Christ. He quietly prayed during that critical time in his life as I read to him some of my favorite Psalms, as well as John's Gospel. When I pushed him around the hospital corridors, he spontaneously shared with me his thoughts about life and death—and the many sticking points in between. On another occasion, I arrived at Andre's house just hours after he had faced something extraordinarily difficult in his life; he collapsed physically and emotionally before my eyes. I put him to bed and stayed near at hand for two days. He bounced back, of course, wiser and with more understanding of what he and, by extension, others were capable of enduring.

Andre's six children were always a constant source of blessings to him, and as adults they remained close to both father and mother. When his three oldest children married (Suzanne at the home of a friend on a private island off of Portland, Maine; Andre in a Greek Orthodox church, and Jeb in the backyard of the bride's parents' home), he felt that in many ways he had been a better father than he sometimes imagined. After the publication of *The Cage Keeper and Other Stories* (1989), written by son Andre, I organized a reception and dinner party at America House. Andre clearly took delight in his son's literary achievement, and in knowing he would receive more and more recognition in the years to come, though, alas, he did not lived long enough to hear the public praise for *House of Sand and Fog*. Not surprisingly, Andre was always at great peace during Catholic liturgies, as I can personally attest to, whether in the chapel of America House, in a parish church, or in his home in Haverhill; they provided him an opportunity to reflect on the myriad gifts he had received, however unsolicited, what he had done with them, and how he should avail himself of them in the future.

Though it would be easy to think that after three marriages and three divorces, in addition to a life-altering accident that initially cast him into great darkness, Andre would have allowed his nether self to become dominant. But this was not the case. He was very much aware of life's conjunctural blessings, so much so that he rose, sometimes anxiously and hesitatingly, above any negativity that could too easily envelop him. His literary output is testimony enough to the dogged discipline one expects of a former Marine:

The Lieutenant (novel, 1967)
Separate Flights (stories, 1975)
Adultery and Other Choices (stories, 1977)
Finding a Girl in America (stories, 1980)
The Times Are Never So Bad: A Novella and Eight Stories (1983)
Voices from the Moon (novel, 1984)
We Don't Live Here Anymore: Four Novellas (1984)
The Last Worthless Evening: Four Novellas and Two Stories (1986)
Selected Stories (1988)
Broken Vessels (essays, 1991)
Dancing After Hours (stories, 1996)
Meditations From a Movable Chair (essays, 1998)

Dubus brought the totality of his own experiences to his fiction, but not in some overtly biographical way. While a number of Dubus' essays are autobiographical in nature ("Letter to a Writers' Workshop," "Digging," "A Hemingway Story," "Mailer at the Algonquin," "Brother," "Bodily Mysteries," "A Country Road Song," "Carrying," "Liv Ullman in Spring," "Love in the Morning," and "Giving Up the Gun," to name a few), his stories and novellas never *seem* far removed from the ambit of his immediate experience—an insight confirmed to me by his son, Andre, who agreed that his father was basing a certain amount of his fiction on his own life, as well as on the lives of the men and women, handicapped in one way or not, he knew in and around Haverhill:

> I sing of those who cannot. To view human suffering as an abstraction, as a statement about how plucky we all are, is to blow air through brass while the boys and girls march in parade off to war. Seeing the flesh as only a challenge to the spirit is as false as seeing the spirit as only a challenge to the flesh. On the planet are people with whole and strong bodies, whose wounded spirits need the constant help that the quadriplegic needs for his body. What we need is not the sound of horns rising to the sky, but the steady beat of the bass drum. When you march to a bass drum, your left foot touches the earth with each beat, and you can feel the drum in your body: *boom* and *boom* and *boom* and *pity people pity people pity people*. ("Song of Pity")

While in the process of writing he could test the validity of what he was trying to figure out, to see, as he once mentioned to me, if his fiction rang true, like a fork hitting finely leaded glass. Andre had perfect literary pitch; he often taped his stories and then listened to them in order to assess their coherence and veracity.

Andre once related to me on a calm fall afternoon in 1985, while both of us were sitting in rocking chairs sipping Jack Daniels on his front porch in Tuscaloosa, Alabama, where he was writer-in-residence at the university, the axis upon which his fiction rotated:

> Well, I see the whole world as a Catholic, so I can't help but see my characters through the eyes of a Catholic . . . I've seen the whole of my fictive world through the eyes of someone who believes the main problem in the United States is that we have lost all spiritual values and not replaced them with anything that is comparable.

Granted, Flannery O'Connor could have spoken the exact same words, though her works are more an effort *to recover* the ideal of the Holy in an age in which both the meaning and reality of the concept have been obscured. I have always felt Andre did something quite different, as articulated, among other places, in his fine essay "On Charon's Wharf."

While O'Connor and Dubus both believed that the loss of the Holy involved for society a concomitant loss of depth and subsequent diminution, O'Connor felt the need to journey through the radically profane, embracing evil at times in order to rediscover the good; she often relied on a sequence of aphorisms and clichés spoken by her protagonists (those in "Good Country People" illustrate this well), which, when taken as a whole, provide tremendous spiritual and sacramental insight. Her narratives have, at times, an instructive, formulaic, catechetical dimension to them, most likely motivated by a desperate desire to affirm a basis for human existence that transcends the waywardness and willfulness of the individual human self. O'Connor excels at bringing a character, as she does with Mrs. McIntyre in "The Displaced Person," to an elusive moment of decision, and allowing that person to remain suspended before our eyes.

Dubus' fiction, on the other hand, *re-presents* most often the pang and tether of marital situations that take their own natural course in such ways that a reader might feel that the author witnessed the action of the story, but did not direct it. Because of Dubus' view of the sacramentality of life, the Holy is never separated from the deepest recesses of his fictional characters, much in the spirit of Gerard Manley Hopkins' famous lines from "God's Grandeur": "The world is charged with the grandeur of God. / It will flame out, like shining from shook foil; / It gathers to a greatness, like the ooze of oil / crushed." And, as implied, the "crushing" can have unexpectedly devastating results. While Dubus' devotional writings—utterly sincere, but curiously lacking the natural-ness of his fiction—focus usually on his love of Christ in the Eucharist, his broader sacramental bias, as expressed in his essay "Sacraments," emerges from passions one could not imagine O'Connor expressing:

> Making love can be a sacrament, if our souls are as naked as our bodies, if our souls are in harmony with our bodies, and through our bodies are embracing each other in love and fear and trembling, knowing that this act could be the beginning of a third human being, if we are a man and a woman; knowing that the roots and trunk of death are within each of us, and that one of its branches may block or rupture an artery as we kiss.

Dubus' fiction often revolves around sexual liaisons, certainly not to titillate his readers, but to reaffirm a fundamental human drive through which we can intimately unite ourselves with another. As his friend Tobias Wolff wrote about Dubus in the introduction to *Broken Vessels*,

> He is one of the few fiction writers around who writes well about love—not just about lost love, either, in the moping nostalgic manner, but about love before it is lost, love as it is experienced, in whatever form it takes. He is the only writer who has ever made me feel the love of a teenage boy for God, or the love of a teenage girl for the cigarette she is smoking.

Dubus knew that human intercourse can at times be violent and at other times tender, yet always it involves a desire to seek satisfaction, never complete on this earth, but lying, he sometimes suggests, just beyond the horizon of our earthly existence. Yet, one could well ask what will ultimately happen to Miranda in "Miranda Over the Valley," after her initial sexual experiences have left her empty and sad. As the great mystics have shown repeatedly, even when the divine hand seems absent, it is not, though one episode or story or novella might not locate it with any precision.

Walker Percy told me more than once that he never really wanted to write about God and evil and salvation in his fiction (though he did so in a number of his essays) because his readers would become suspicious and put down his fiction. Who would read novels, he believed, that contain inspirational messages? Dubus understood Percy's dilemma, but addressed the issue both more directly and more obliquely, in that his New England folk are involved in a dramatic struggle simply to exist, often in trying circumstances, though without any trepidation of being dislocated by either the explicit presence or the apparent absence of the Holy, as depicted in his masterly "A Father's Story." Rather Dubus' genius seems more preoccupied with probing the mundane questions Peter Jackman asks in "The Winter Father": How many conversations can one have through windshields and how many times must a father endure the shutting of doors as children enter or leave one's house?

More than any writer I have read, Dubus unites his home and church language with his out-of-home and out-of-church language. He speaks and writes with one voice, which certain Catholics might find theologically unsettling, much as they would reject the presence of a thrice-divorced Catholic at the communion rail. How can one be a devout Catholic faithful to the Eucharist while canonically (it would seem) being outside the fold? A serious question, demanding a serious response. Just as Dubus struggled with this question in his heart, so too he struggled to portray—while writing one clear sentence after another—the morally fretted dilemmas facing his fictional characters, though never, I believe, to demonstrate a religious insight or position. Rather, as has been noted by a number of critics, he constructs fiction that often involves the building up and the breaking down of human relationships, even depicting lingering sadness, as in "A Love Song," which, at times, asymptotically approaches despair, but finally is never despairing. And sometimes, as in "Blessings," families survive intact.

To stand in Dubus' presence, or to receive phone calls from him about issues he had to face, was to be assured of your own freedom. His characters, too, are free to choose over and over and over again—and Dubus as author portrays forthrightly their plights (however disturbing they may be—not excluding premarital and extramarital sex, abortion, death from AIDS, and attempted and accidental murder), all the while refraining from making preemptive decisions one way or another about the morality of what is happening. The exquisite conclusion to "The Colonel's Wife," which resolves the infidelities of wheel-chair-bound Robert Townsend and his beautiful, free-spirited wife Lydia, shows the unspoken resolutions in life Dubus admired:

> He knew this: sunlight on the twist of lemon in her glass as she lifted it by the stem and brought it to her red lips. On the day the snow fell till midnight, she made no promises, and had not asked any of him. He did not want promises. They were words and feelings wafting about in a season he or Lydia may not live to see. He wanted only to know what had happened and what was happening now, to see that: brilliant as the sky, not as the sun, bright as Lydia's eyes.

As an intrepid searcher himself, as a fictional truth-sayer, Dubus attempted throughout his life to correlate what he intuited or knew with what he witnessed around him, or as St. Augustine put it in describing truth, to have one's intellect conform to reality, to affirm that which is.

I last saw Andre Dubus during the weekend he had come to New York to celebrate the publication of his last book, *Meditations from a*

Movable Chair. A small group of his friends (Philip Spitzer, his agent; Phil's daughter Anne-Lise; Marion Ettlinger, a noted photographer; Jack Herlihy, who usually accompanied Andre on the road; plus some editors from Knopf and myself) gathered—as we usually did whenever Andre was in town—one muggy night at Sushiya on West 56th Street. Andre thoroughly enjoyed bringing people together (didn't he want to follow in three magnificent novellas the lives of his own fictional creatures—Edith and Hank Allison, Jack and Terry Linhart, and Joe Ritchie?). On this hot, muggy night he was exuberant, despite any discomfort he felt in negotiating between table legs. Eventually, he positioned his wheelchair near the almost full-length front windows, which had been opened to provide for some ventilation. At one point a Scandinavian couple passed by and stopped, astonished to see this packet of Americans eating boatloads of sushi, yakitori, sashimi, and oshinko. They stood for a long time conversing with Andre, whom I am sure was entertaining them with stories of one sort or another. As I watched I thought: This is why we work, to come together for dinners like this. Andre had that knack of holding the attention of his listeners and readers. He was a dear friend and I know I will never see the likes of him again.

Patrick Samway, S.J., the MacLean Professor of English at Saint Joseph's University in Philadelphia, Pennsylvania, is the author of a book on Faulkner and *Walker Percy: A Life*, listed by the *New York Times* as a "notable book" of 1997. He has edited *Signposts in a Strange Land*, a collection of Percy's speeches and essays, and *A Thief of Peirce: The Letters of Kenneth Laine Ketner and Walker Percy*. In addition, he has co-edited four anthologies of Southern literature. Father Samway has had a number of visiting professorships, as well as two teaching Fulbrights in France (University of Nantes and the University of Paris VII). Most recently, he has been the Will and Ariel Durant Professor of Humanities at Saint Peter's College in Jersey City, New Jersey.

Brian Hanley

Andre Dubus amidst the Critics

> It is . . . the task of criticism to establish principles; to improve opinion into knowledge; and to distinguish those means of pleasing which depend upon known causes and rational deduction, from the nameless and inexplicable elegancies which appeal wholly to the fancy, from which we feel delight, but know not how they produce it, and which may well be termed the enchantresses of the soul.
> —Samuel Johnson, *Rambler* 92

> It is advantageous to an author, that his book should be attacked as well as praised. Fame is a shuttlecock. If it be struck only at one end of the room, it will soon fall to the ground. To keep it up, it must be struck at both ends.
> —Samuel Johnson to Sir John Dalrymple, 1773[1]

The outlook on criticism expressed here by Samuel Johnson seems particularly apt in surveying Andre Dubus' literary reputation for a couple of reasons. To begin with, the work of Andre Dubus, like that of Johnson, attracted a vast amount of contemporaneous criticism which grew in quantity with the publication of each successive work. Some 3,500 individual publications that at least mention Johnson appeared during his lifetime, so Johnson's understanding of the critic's place was based on, among other things, a fairly broad inventory of first-hand experience as the subject of both worthy and dull-witted criticism.[2] Reviews of Dubus' work are not nearly so numerous, but research based on queries of *Lexis/Nexis, Humanities Abstracts, Book Review Digest,* and other sources, turns up hundreds of individual commentaries—the great majority book reviews—on Dubus' fiction between the mid-1970s and

1997, two years before Dubus died. Indeed, Dubus' final collection of short stories, *Dancing After Hours* (Knopf, 1996), brought forth something on the order of 100 reviews; the *New York Times* alone offered three separate reviews, one by Richard Bausch (25 February 1996), the others by Christopher Lehmann-Haupt (14 March) and Mel Gussow (23 March). *Time* allocated nearly seven hundred words to a review of *Dancing After Hours*, which is a relatively generous amount of space for serious art. Newspapers large and small from every region of the United States also felt it necessary to give notice to Dubus' collection. Reviews can be found in such places as the *The Providence Journal-Bulletin*, *The Buffalo News*, *The News and Record* (Greensboro, NC), *The Plain Dealer* (Cleveland, OH), *The Milwaukee Journal Sentinel*, *The Kansas City Star*, *The Houston Chronicle*, *The Ledger* (Lakeland, FL), *The Denver Post*, *The Seattle Times*, and *The Fresno Bee*. It scarcely needs mentioning that the work was widely reviewed in various religious publications such as *America*, *Commonweal*, *The Christian Century*, and the *National Catholic Reporter*. The paperback edition of *Dancing After Hours* appeared in April 1997, some fifteen months after the hardback, and drew at least a dozen reviews in major publications such as the *Chicago Sun-Times* and the *Washington Post*, several of which had carried reviews of the cloth-bound version months earlier.

Dancing After Hours was thus continuously and widely reviewed from January 1996, when *Publishers Weekly* gave notice of the collection a month before its publication, until well into the summer of 1997. Critical attention on this scale is an astounding achievement given the high ratio of newly published works to book reviews. Only some ten percent of new titles nowadays manage to attract even one review. Dubus has thus earned a place with the leading fiction writers of our day whose newly published short stories seem to concentrate the intelligence of the literary world.

Johnson's understanding of the proper relation between author and critic is also relevant to Dubus' literary career because what Johnson says illuminates nicely the predicament Dubus' reputation as a writer of short fiction now seems to face. Andre Dubus on the whole has been treated sympathetically by critics, reviewers, and scholars, but not quite in the way he most surely deserves. True enough, here and there one comes across a discerning piece of criticism—the reviews of his work by Richard Bausch, Joyce Carol Oates, and John Updike, for instance—but in truth the bulk of what is written about Dubus must be categorized as appreciative if a bit insubstantial, offering little of merit for future generations of scholars to build on. Much of the commentary on Dubus is favorable—but rarely does this material transcend the quality of the basic summary followed by lofty but nonspecific praise of the kind that makes for gripping dust jacket blurbs but not for the sort criticism that outlasts contemporary fame.[3] What little unfavorable commentary that does exist can be dismissed as pettifogging or obtuse.

For an example of the kind of literary criticism that Dubus' fiction truly deserves given his literary achievements, one need only consider the rigorous debate over Alexander Pope's reputation in the four decades following his death in 1744, which was actuated by Joseph Warton's depreciative appraisal of Pope's poetry (*An Essay on the Writings and Genius of Pope*, 1756) and sustained by Samuel Johnson's apologetic commentary in his *Lives of the Poets* (1779-81). What we find here are two first-rate authors arguing over the direction a lately dead literary icon has taken poetry. In drawing on the literary heritage of the preceding seventy-five years or so as they defined and then weighed the merits of Augustan and Romantic poetics, both Johnson and Warton created the most enduring sort of literary criticism. The work of Andre Dubus would reward a similar measure of substantive consideration.

Indeed, it is a pity that Joseph Epstein, an otherwise perceptive and eloquent observer of the contemporary cultural scene, neglected to consider Dubus' work in his collection of essays, *Plausible Prejudices: Essays on American Writing* (1985), which argues that today's literary culture is "second-rate," and "considerably less good than it ought to be."[4] Equally disappointing is that neither the fortnightly *National Review* nor *The Weekly Standard*, which employs Epstein as a contributing editor, bothered to review *Dancing After Hours*. Both of these publications offer readers book reviewing of a very high standard. Dubus' essentially conservative social outlook, the aesthetic excellence of his short fiction and, at least as far as William F. Buckley's *National Review* is concerned, Dubus' Catholic sensibility, should have drawn full, sympathetic notices from both magazines. The *National Review* in particular would have been an especially worthy forum for a mature consideration of Dubus' achievement on a couple of counts. First, because the intellectual standing of *National Review* is of such eminence as to attract authors and critics of the finest caliber. The *National Review*'s 24 January 2000 issue, for example, featured essays by, among others, Saul Bellow on the state of literature, Robert Conquest on the West, Paul

Johnson on the arts, and Jean-Francois Revel on democracy. Second, reviewers in Mr. Buckley's magazine are generally given room to evaluate their subjects that is just ample enough to carry criticism that might prove to be of lasting value.

Criticism of Dubus' short fiction naturally falls into two forms. A discussion of Dubus' reputation in the scholarly community can be surveyed by consulting the Gale Group's online *Literature Resource Center*. Of course, the Twayne Series offers a volume on Dubus' short fiction by Thomas E. Kennedy (1988); Dubus enthusiasts will be interested in this volume chiefly because of its interviews and judicious selection of criticism—including excerpts from reviews by John Updike and Joyce Carol Oates. There are a dozen or so scholarly articles and even a pair of doctoral dissertations on Dubus, but most of these are of no particular value to the general reader. What I find most disappointing here is that the influence of Catholicism on Dubus' fiction has not received the careful and full scholarly attention that the subject deserves.

Only a handful of articles exist that explore expressions of faith in Dubus' fiction manage to do so in an intelligent yet sympathetic manner; the remainder are to be read with at least some measure of skepticism. One article on Dubus, for instance, refers to the Catholic Church's "sexual politics," a term heavily freighted with ignorance of the institution it professes to explain.[5] By contrast, John B. Breslin's essay, "Playing Out the Patterns of Sin and Grace," in *Commonweal*, offers a neat survey of the Catholic underpinnings of Dubus' fiction, but he also clarifies the broader humane appeal of these works. "Dubus accepts our flawed condition as a given, but he manages to view his characters' failings with a compassion that bespeaks an equal conviction that grace is powerfully at work in the world," Breslin argues. "In a number of stories this pattern of sin and grace is played out within a specifically Catholic setting, but just as often, the characters have no religious convictions or, at most, exhibit a vestigial sensibility of the divine in lives otherwise determined by an overtly secular culture."[6] Breslin here illuminates an important feature of Dubus' literary art. The general reader can derive pleasure and instruction from Dubus' short fiction, but astute Catholic readers will discover that Dubus' short fiction enriches their faith.

In fact, what is needed is a book-length study that includes Dubus in a survey of Catholicism in fiction since, say, World War II. The setting and characterization of Evelyn Waugh's novel *Brideshead Revisited* could scarcely be more remote from the industrial neighborhoods outside of

Boston portrayed in Dubus' fiction and the flawed, often bewildered working-class people who inhabit his stories. Nevertheless, Dubus' short fiction and Waugh's novel are united by the same basic outlook on the Church's relation with, among other things, the materialism of the modern world. The theme of *Brideshead Revisited*—"the operation of divine grace on a group of diverse but closely connected characters," as Waugh himself put the matter—works well as the underlying subject of much of Dubus' short fiction. A particularly good expression of this idea can be found in Dubus' story, "Miranda Over the Valley."[7]

"Miranda Over the Valley" explores the trauma an unmarried eighteen-year-old college freshman goes through as she is browbeaten into getting an abortion by her parents, boyfriend, and roommate. The characters are marvelously drawn: her tormentors are shallow, self-centered, materialistic, but they also retain a measure of common humanity—not for a moment do we think of them as mere ciphers. The dramatic tension of the story centers on Miranda's mental anguish as she is led to do something that the story itself would have us believe is a gross affront to her native moral sense, and which leaves her emotionally damaged in the aftermath. "It was not remorse she felt. It was dying," Miranda thinks to herself after the abortion. "Already she would not think June when she knew she would say: Today is probably the day my baby would have been born. So she could not be alone anymore, not even in this apartment she loved, this city she loved."[8] "Miranda Over the Valley" is a masterpiece of short fiction. The story, along with "Falling in Love" in *Dancing After Hours*, expresses Church teaching in ways that no political tract can ever match, no matter how closely argued, but the story does so without a trace of sanctimony or self-congratulatory piety. Dubus once said that "Miranda" is "full of all sorts of religious symbols . . . which I stuck in for my own reasons and hoped that no reader would ever discover."[9] For Catholic readers such as myself, the symbols are perhaps not quite as inconspicuous as Dubus assumed. Even so, the story contains enough ambiguity—Miranda's parents, ultimately, are actuated by love for their daughter; Miranda herself is no gestating martyr to her faith—to avoid the sort of didacticism that might put off non-religious readers.

The dearth of mature studies that explain the Catholic underpinnings of Dubus' short fiction is matched by the inadequacy of scholarship that seeks to shed light on Dubus' work within the history of ideas. Dubus' literary achievement thus far has been evaluated in academic circles almost entirely by the lights of modish critical theory. But what Dubus deserves is scholarship that illuminates the place of his fiction within what Mortimer Adler describes as the "Great Conversation." My own view is that Dubus' work, among other things, explores the necessity of suffering in the acquisition of wisdom—as do the *Oedipus* plays by Sophocles and Shakespeare's *King Lear*. Needless to say, there is a Catholic element present in Dubus' treatment of the subject—that suffering purifies—but Dubus often makes the case from a predominantly secular point of view that prudence, humility, and benevolence are best taught by the chastening hand of experience.

> Nothing is more delightful than to possess well fortified sanctuaries serene, built up by the teachings of the wise, whence you may look down from the height upon others and behold them all astray, wandering abroad and seeking the path of life: — The strife of wits, the fight for precedence, all labouring night and day with surpassing toil to mount upon the pinnacle of riches and to lay hold on power. O pitiable minds of men, O blind intelligences! In what gloom of life, in how great perils is passed all your poor span of time![10]

Lucretius' commentary here captures nicely the relation between Dubus, his readers, and the characters in his fiction. The short stories of Andre Dubus place readers in a position of advantage—we know the thoughts of characters without being beholden to their passions or unduly influenced, as they are, by their social and moral environment—thus allowing us to observe and learn from men and women whose misbegotten understanding of happiness and self-fulfillment leads them to bedevil their lives.

Every story in *Dancing After Hours* at least touches upon the relation between wisdom and suffering, but I found "Falling in Love" and "The Lover" to be particularly affecting. Dubus here offers us a pair of exemplums that help us understand the vast chasm that separates mere sexual gratification from love. In fact, Dubus' point in these two stories is obvious enough: at an historical moment when chastity and self-restraint have been characterized as bad things—the pernicious superstitions of our pious ancestors, as Hugh Hefner might put the matter—and that happiness is to be found in sexual liberation, Dubus instructs us otherwise. Both Ted in "Falling in Love" and Lee in "The Lover" suffer greatly as they move from blind acceptance of modernity's outlook on sexuality to a fuller, more humane understanding of love in all its manifestations. Love as Ted and Lee initially understand it amounts to what Dubus would have us believe to be an iniquitous parody of the idea, an expression of brutal selfishness rather than the mutual and unreserved affection that can be shared between a man and a woman. Of course, Dubus himself was thrice married, thrice divorced. Perhaps through his fiction Dubus tries to realize the emotional contentment that, for whatever reasons, his own marriages never quite managed to bring to maturity.

In "Falling In Love," Susan Dorsey, the live-in girlfriend of disabled Vietnam War veteran Ted Briggs, falls pregnant. The affair begins in what must be thought of as typical for the hedonistic 1970s: the two meet at a party, spend the night together, and remain a couple, sharing the same apartment. When Susan breaks the news to Ted of her pregnancy, he asks her to marry him and, failing that, to at least carry the child to term so that he can rear the baby by himself. "I'm twenty-two years old, I'm going to New York, and you want me to have a fucking baby?" Susan says. "Not a fucking baby. Our baby, Susan. Our baby," Ted responds, antagonizing Susan further. At lunch with his friend Nick some time later, Ted tries to make sense of matters. "From where the sun stands now I will ejaculate no more forever in the body of a woman who will kill our child," Ted declares, "and saying it," the narrator tells us, Ted "released all the grief, as something he felt he could see, touch, in the air before his face, and now he felt only rage, and the strength and conviction it brings." Nick advises him to date women who use contraceptives. "Ted looked at him, tossed his cane onto the couch, and held Nick's arm. He said, 'The pill isn't a philosophy. I need a philosophy to go out there with. I can't just go out there with a cock, and a heart. Maybe I need a wife.' "[11] By the lights of the sexual revolution—in which copulation is released from the burdens of procreation or marriage, and physical abuse and venereal infection never enter the picture—Ted's romance should have been immensely rewarding. But the affair with Susan has yielded great suffering which, in the end, allows Ted to become wiser. Indeed, by the end of the story we find that his moral intelligence has matured; Ted can discriminate between love in its transcendent forms, which he aches for, and the psychic and emotional vacuity of merely coaxing an orgasm out of his body.

"The Lover" explores the desiccated emotional life of Lee, a "fifty-five-year-old restaurant manager," a three-times-divorced father of five. The bulk of the story is taken up by an interior monologue in which Lee tries to come to terms with his loneliness. Even though at the beginning of the story Lee comes very close to justifying the mess he's made of his life, there is very much a permanent air of regret and disconsolation hanging over his self-communion.

> Lee was on good terms with the two mothers of his children [the third wife forced him to get a vasectomy]; time had healed him, had allowed him to forget whatever he and the women had done to each other, or removed the precision of pain from his memory . . . sometimes he wished as a boy does: that in some way his first marriage had never ended, yet his second had occurred so the daughter and son from that one would be on earth; and that he and the two women and five children were one family.

Lee goes on to have a liaison with nubile Doreen, a nineteen-year-old employee of his, but instead of stimulating his sense of virility, the affair plunges him further into despair. In a post-coital dialogue with Doreen, who is every bit his equal in matters social and moral, Lee begins to grope toward the root of his agony and the suffering he has caused others.

> Somewhere I missed something. Something my cock can't feel. Even my heart can't feel. Something that keeps you from fucking while sharks are eating your neighbors; while one is coming for you. I broke the hearts of three wives. It's not what I set out to do. . . . I ripped childhood from five children. It'll always be with them, that pain. Like joints that hurt when it rains. There's more to it, but I can't find it. It's not walking with a cane and giving cigar rings to grandchildren.[12]

Lee begins the story as a self-indulgent man whose moral complacency is aggravated by self-pity, but by the closing paragraph Lee at least gestures toward self-awareness. What we see here is a man who, by modernity's creed of sexual liberation, should have been very much pleased with himself. Lee manages to escape from marriages that, however satisfying they may have been initially, grow stale after a time. Nevertheless, Lee's heedless pursuit of self-gratification has driven him to pursue a state of contentment even as he stubbornly despises the only means to that end, a truth he doesn't fully apprehend until the end of the story—when all he can do is ruminate on the flotsam scattered in the wake of his cramped understanding of the relation between sexual desire and love. As the story comes to a close, Lee realizes that his selfishness has infected what started out as two happy marriages and driven him into a plainly unsuitable third one. At the close of "The Lover," Dubus endows Lee with a moral vision he lacked earlier; the tragic element here is that a considerable weight of suffering and regret must accompany his newly acquired wisdom.

Hundreds of reviews have been written about Andre Dubus' work, but very few offer probing commentary of the sort that informs literary taste. There are several reasons for this state of affairs, the chief being that reviewers for the most part are manacled by the demands of time and space. Surveying the dozens of reviews of Dubus' *Dancing After Hours*, for instance, one is struck by the underlying sameness of the commentary. Most reviewers comment on Dubus' 1986 accident that put him in a wheelchair, for instance, and take note of his carefully drawn characters from the blue-collar world, and so on. In fact, many of the reviews of *Dancing After Hours* say basically the same thing about the same set of stories—"The Colonel's Wife" expresses Dubus' private suffering, as do the Ted Briggs stories; the LuAnn Arceneaux narratives touch upon the influence of grace in everyday lives, even as they offer an unvarnished comment on the promiscuity that was encouraged by the counter-culture of the 1960s.

Generally speaking, these reviewers offer praise of the sort that works nicely as advertising copy but, without explanatory comment, contributes little to a mature appreciation of Dubus' literary achievement. Take for instance the lead sentence of the review in the *Stuart News/Port St. Lucie News* (Stuart, FL), 30 March 1996. Andre Dubus "is the best Catholic storyteller since Graham Greene," the Andrew M. Greeley Religion News Service claims. "In some ways, Dubus is even more Catholic than Greene because grace is more obvious in his stories and hope is far more powerful." Such a thesis might serve well as the organizing principle of an entire volume—or as a dust jacket blurb. But no book review can deliver on such claims; in fact, Greene is never again mentioned in the remainder of the 600-word commentary that follows. Obviously, Dubus enthusiasts should temper their expectations of rank-and-file reviewers because they don't have the time properly to study the work of art they are criticizing. In some instances the haste with which some reviews are written produces the most embarrassing mistakes. The Greensboro, North Carolina *News & Record* (14 April 1996) briefly surveyed the story "The Intruder" in *Dancing After Hours*, but referred to it as "Predators."

In most cases, however, reviewers may touch upon a profoundly important feature of Dubus' literary art without pausing to consider the full significance of their discovery—much like the German tribal warrior in Julius Caesar's *Commentaries* who, following a successful raid on a Roman settlement, discarded the gold coins he found in a Roman commander's lodgings even as he retained the sack they were carried in, thinking the weathered and worn bit of leather to be of much greater value. The review of *Dancing After Hours* by Sean Kinch in the *Austin-American Statesman* (17 March 1996) is a good example of the thwarted promise one finds in most reviews of Dubus' work. "As a sociological document, *Dancing After Hours* offers glimpses into the changes in American sexual practices over the past twenty-five years. The earliest stories are set in the 1970s, when sexual involvement required little deliberation," Kinch writes. "In the later stories, set in the '90s, the characters debate internally about the advantages of sex vs. the threat of disease, and when they do go to bed they bring along a condom, that ubiquitous metonymy for safe sex."

Kinch merely scratches the surface here. In *Dancing After Hours*, Dubus treats the massive repudiation of traditional sexual norms that began in the 1950s and that continues in our own day as all of one piece and evaluates the effects of the sexual revolution by the lights of his Catholic faith. The carnal incontinence of his characters is set forth as emotionally self-destructive but not absolutely evil; a thing more to be pitied and rued rather than excoriated. Dubus' characters do not seek to justify their concupiscence by way of carefully constructed reasoning—which would mean that, at least for the characters who are Catholic, that they had rejected a pillar of their faith. Instead, Dubus' characters behave as they do because they are seeking pure love and latch onto its erotic aspects because it is the most immediate, most alluring, and least demanding— if also the most transitory and treacherous—quality of love.

The constraints of time shackle the reviewer, but so too does the place of publication. The reviews that can move copies of a volume off store bookshelves necessarily appear in general-interest magazines and newspapers. But getting reviewed in such venues means that space is a premium. A horseback calculation tells me that reviews in most places must be kept to, say, fewer than nine hundred words. Feature-length reviews in magazines such as the *National Review* rarely stray much beyond two thousand words or so. Obviously, the critic who means to shape literary taste with a book review must severely limit the range of analysis. John Updike and Joyce Carol Oates have reviewed Dubus' work, as has Richard Bausch. But however perceptive their observations, their commentary cannot help but be shaped by the word limits imposed by the *New York Times Review of Books* and the *New Yorker*, which must appeal to a fairly wide range of interests.

Basically, the reviews by Updike, Oates, and Bausch succeed because of the status of their authors. In fact, these authors do the literary world an important service by assuring us that Dubus' literary art does indeed live up to the glowing if generalized praise one finds in the reviews carried by the regional newspapers. In his brief *New Yorker* review of Dubus' novella, "Voices from the Moon," Updike not only encourages us to think of Dubus' fiction as an appealing alternative to the theory-dominated literature and criticism that had already gained a consider-able measure of stature by the mid-eighties, when this review was written—"How rare it is these days, to encounter characters with wills, with a sense of choice"—but Updike also gives his readers an apprecia-tive and eloquent summation of the place of Catholicism in the lives of Dubus' characters. For "Mr. Dubus, amid the self-seeking tangle of secular America, the Church still functions as a standard measure, a repository of mysteries that can give scale and structure to our social lives."[13] Joyce Carol Oates offers a similarly discerning if rather austere commentary on Dubus' 1983 collection, *The Times Are Never So Bad*. "Though Mr. Dubus' characters are not precisely 'good'—most of them perform criminal actions of one kind or another—we are allowed to see how they define themselves as other than merely 'bad' through the author's extraordinary sympathy with them." The stories, she adds, are "really triumphs of voice, memorable for their resonance." What gives Ms. Oates' review a measure of interest is its evenhandedness. Apart from the novella, "The Pretty Girl," the stories here "are somewhat under-devel-oped, even sketchy. On the whole, *The Times Are Never So Bad* comprises "spare pieces of fiction, willfully pruned, it seems, of the rich and idiosyncratic details that elsewhere make Mr. Dubus' writing so good; they read rather more like excerpts from longer works than stories com-plete in themselves." Writing in the *New York Times Book Review* (25

February 1996), Richard Bausch asserts that the story "Dancing After Hours" is "one of the most gracious and exquisite works of fiction I have ever read." Needless to say, all of this makes for a very powerful endorsement. Nevertheless, because of the cramped confines of modern book reviewing the reader unfamiliar with Dubus' art may find himself aching for extended analysis. Of course, such is largely the duty of the scholar, and only the passage of time will tell if the academic world meets its responsibilities adequately.

Perhaps an appropriate way to close this essay is to offer my own tribute to Andre Dubus. One of the best of Dubus' short stories, in my view, is "The Intruder." Like the best short fiction, there is more going on here than is apparent at first glance. With his spare prose, Dubus manages to offer a probing analysis of the psychology of an adolescent boy who makes a dreadful mistake without encouraging us to despise him; in fact, I at least sympathize with the protagonist. "The Intruder" tells of a homicide committed by thirteen-year-old Kenneth, the younger child of Mr. and Mrs. Girard. The Girards go out for the evening and leave Kenneth in the care of his older sister Connie. Connie's boyfriend Douglas drops by but leaves shortly afterward on the implicit understanding that he is to return once Kenneth has gone to bed. Kenneth later shoots Douglas with his hunting rifle just as Douglas approaches Connie's window, on the plausible assumption that Douglas is a prowler. The precise extent of Kenneth's culpability in the murder remains cloudy not only for circumstantial reasons—on his return Douglas does lurk about the house much as a malefactor would—but also on the more significant grounds that Kenneth can't tell the difference between reality and his imagination, an unhappy circumstance that has grown out of the boy's desperate loneliness aggravated by his adolescence and by his emotional estrangement from his parents. At some level, perhaps, Kenneth had allowed for the possibility that the intruder was Connie's boyfriend—but his pulling the trigger does not appear to have been a deliberate act of murder. Rather, Kenneth's apprehension of Douglas' return was one of a piece with his outing in the forest earlier that day: "he lifted his twenty-two-caliber rifle and fired at a rusty tin can across the creek, the can becoming a Nazi face in a window as he squeezed the trigger and voices filled him: *You got him, Captain. You got him.*" Clearly, Kenneth's imagination at the moment of decision led him to understand his actions as chivalric rather than vicious.[14]

In important ways, Kenneth is a typical adolescent boy. He craves admiration. He wants to make his life significant through courage, self-sacrifice, physical prowess—a yearning that finds expression in the fantasies that center on the exploits of the commando, the western gunfighter, the sports hero. Needless to say, this idea is as old as the literature of the West—the *Iliad*, after all, centers on the youthful Achilles' search for significance before the universe. Telemachus, just out of his teens, strives to become the equal of his long-lost father in *The Odyssey*. Peruse Lord Chesterfield's letters to his son and you shall see a father attempting to sharpen this instinct by unceasingly exhorting the adolescent Philip Stanhope to cut a dashing figure in the world: "can there be a greater pleasure than to be universally allowed to excel those of one's own age and manner of life?," Chesterfield writes to his son. "And, consequently, can there be anything more mortifying than to be excelled by them?"[15]

Kenneth's conflation of imagination and reality, commonplace as such habits of mind can be at that age, is not in itself disquieting. What is so troubling is that Kenneth indulges these fantasies not out of the exuberance of the young boy looking forward to the challenges of manhood but as a way of medicating his aching yet unexpressed and scarcely acknowledged sense of alienation and inadequacy. We learn, for instance, that other boys his age despise him; we also are told of Kenneth's ineptitude at sports, something which deeply embarrasses him—particularly when he is introduced to Connie's athletic boyfriends. Kenneth relishes Connie's abundant, unqualified fondness for him, but her sisterly affection ultimately evokes in Kenneth self-loathing. "He believed that Connie thought he was exactly like her, that he was talkative and well liked. But she never saw him with his classmates. He felt that he was deceiving her."

Of equal importance is that Kenneth's parents don't seem to make any effort to understand their son, which finds its most baneful expression in their breezy indifference to his gun-toting expeditions into the woods. It might be argued that Kenneth's behavior escapes the notice of his parents because what he does must have seemed very ordinary for a boy growing up in the South at an historical moment—the late 1950s, early 1960s—when it was yet possible to buy a Browning A-5 auto-loading shotgun or a Remington Wingmaster 870 pump-action from the Sears & Roebuck mail order catalogue—for fifty dollars or less. But we must remember that the solitude of Kenneth's shooting expedition is its defining aspect, and this could only have been viewed as irregular or foreboding under any circumstances. Surely the shooting sports were then viewed, as they are now, as an essentially social activity, between fathers and sons in particular. Witness the inter-generational bonding that hunting fosters between Joe and Aleck in Caroline Gordon's story, "The Last Day in the Field." Glance at any recent hunting or shooting publication and you'll see advertisements for firearms or ammunition that emphasize the camaraderie of these activities. The warmth of feeling between father and son generated by the shooting sports is often given heavy emphasis in these ads.

Indeed, what is at least partially the cause of Kenneth's tragedy here is that his parents—his father most especially—remain aloof, a remote presence in his life at a time when their pastoral interest should be at its most intense. The opening sentence of the story makes this point clearly enough. "Because Kenneth Girard loved his parents and his sister and because he could not tell them why he went to the woods, his first moments there were always uncomfortable ones, as if he had left the house to commit a sin." When Kenneth returns from the woods, his parents practically take no notice of him, talking past him at his sister as they tell of their plans of going out for the evening. After dinner, they smoke their cigarettes, study a volume of *Readers' Digest Condensed Books* or glance at the newspaper, leaving Kenneth to himself. Given his tender age, Kenneth is extremely vulnerable to allowing his unsatisfying day-to-day world to become obscured by the self-flattering conceits he entertains; the absence of older brothers or a circle of friends to turn to makes his situation all the worse. Kenneth's suffering should have been abated or erased by the love of his parents, in particular by the devoted attention of his father—but clearly they cannot be bothered to concern themselves with Kenneth's plight.

Such a reading may strike Freudians, feminists, post-structuralists, and other practitioners of literary theory as insipid or friable, but the story itself points most strongly in this direction—in much the same way as the reader of Shakespeare's *Othello* comes to realize that Iago's wickedly ingenious plot does not pivot on demeaning cultural assumptions about women or Moors. Rather, Iago's gambit would have collapsed under the weight of its implausibility had Othello simply been married to Desdemona for, say, a year or even six months instead of mere matter of days. The best literature—and I believe Dubus' fiction will come to be judged as so—always resists neat or obviously pre-fitted interpretations. What is needed, I believe, is further scholarly study of Dubus—

particularly in the vein of traditional, fact-based philology. The reviewers appreciate Dubus' work, as, more importantly, do his contemporary peers in the Republic of Letters. The burden of transmitting Dubus' literary achievement to future generations now rests with the up and coming generations of scholars.

Notes

[1] *The Yale Edition of the Works of Samuel Johnson*, J. Middendorf, gen. ed. (New Haven: Yale UP, 1958-), IV: 122; *Boswell's Life of Johnson*, ed. G. B. Hill, rev. L. F. Powell (Oxford: Oxford UP, 1964), V: 400.

[2] See Helen Louise McGuffie, *Samuel Johnson in the British Press, 1749-1784: A Chronological Checklist* (New York: Garland, 1976).

[3] Joseph Epstein offers a highly intelligent survey of the distressed state of modern book reviewing in *Plausible Prejudices: Essays on American Writing* (New York: W.W. Norton & Co., 1985), 44-60.

[4] Epstein 15.

[5] Lucy Ferriss, "'Never Truly Members': Andre Dubus' Patriarchal Catholicism," *South Atlantic Review* 31 (1994): 39-54.

[6] John B. Breslin, "Playing Out the Patterns of Sin and Grace," *Commonweal* 105 (1988): 652-56. Also worth reading on this subject is Dian Saderup Monson, "Believing in the Word," *First Things*, April 2000: 20-23, and Thomas E. Kennedy's "The Progress from Hunger to Love: Three Novellas by Andre Dubus," *The Hollins Critic* 24 (February 1987): 2-9.

[7] *Brideshead Revisited* (New York: Knopf, 1993), 1.

[8] Andre Dubus, *Selected Stories* (Boston: Godine, 1991), 12-13.

[9] Thomas E. Kennedy, *Andre Dubus: A Study of the Short Fiction* (Boston: Twayne Publishers, 1988), 104-05.

[10] Lucretius, *De Rerum Natura*, W. H. D. Rouse, trans., 3rd ed. (London: Heinemann, 1937), 85.

[11] *Dancing After Hours* (New York: Alfred A. Knopf, 1996), 27-43.

[12] *Dancing After Hours*, 123-38.

[13] John Updike, "Ungreat Lives," *New Yorker*, 4 February 1985, 98.

[14] Dubus, *Dancing After Hours*, 3-19.

[15] *Lord Chesterfield's Letters to His Son and Others* (London: Dent, 1969), 15.

Associate Professor of English at the United States Air Force Academy, **Brian Hanley** is the author of *Samuel Johnson As Book Reviewer: A Duty to Examine the Labours of the Learned* (University of Delaware Press, 2001); his work has appeared in *The New Rambler: The Journal of the Johnson Society of London, American Notes & Queries, War, Literature & The Arts*, and elsewhere.

Thomas G. Bowie, Jr.

Witness to Death and Life:
The Literary Nonfiction of Andre Dubus

> I think it is good for us strangers to be here as witnesses
> to death and life, to prayer and grief.
> —Andre Dubus, "Love in the Morning"

> We are a single human race, whatever our cultural or
> ethnic differences; and yet, as we approach the end of the
> millennium, we seem to be splintering into fragments, each
> with its own political agenda. We seem to be losing a
> spiritual awareness of who and what we are, either as
> individuals or as societies. Memory is responsible for our
> identity; it is the faculty whereby we perceive connections
> between past and present, thus enabling us to make sense
> of our surroundings; it underlies our creative achievements.
> —James McConkey, *The Anatomy of Memory*

Those of us who deeply admire Andre Dubus' fiction have long known
that memory is an enabling faculty underlying his greatest creative
achievements. This is not to say that all his fiction is autobiographical;
indeed, Dubus often wrote stories in order to become someone or something he wasn't, to live lives he never could live himself. Nonetheless, in
a deeply rooted way, memory is responsible for Dubus' identity, whether
we imagine that identity as a father or son in one of his stories, or as a
Catholic writer struggling to reconcile faith with religion, or as a voice
for lower-middleclass New Englanders just hoping to live from day to
day. Dubus is acutely aware of the connections between past and present
that enable him—and us—to make sense of our surroundings. Perhaps
this is a legacy of his southern heritage, a product of his Louisiana
upbringing, or, perhaps more generally, it reveals the pervasive power of

a unique cultural memory—one both powerfully individual and collective—that is a peculiar burden unavoidably associated with living the southern experience, as C. Vann Woodard would have it. Or perhaps such groundedness finds its roots in his distinctly Catholic foundations, with his own twists of course, as critics such as Robert Bellah might suggest.[1] In any event, this quality so often implicit in his fiction, this rooted nature of Dubus' writing that anchors his very identity as an author, becomes explicit in his literary nonfiction. Collecting essays written over the first twenty-five years of his career in the volume *Broken Vessels* (1991), then meditating closely on life lived from a wheelchair in the final years of his life (publishing *Meditations from a Movable Chair* in 1998) Dubus writes some of his most moving work using the form of a personal essay.

"The reality I am watching is moments of grace and skill, gifts received by men who do not turn away from them, but work with them for the few years they are granted."[2] Although Andre Dubus has in mind the particular grace and skill of major league ballplayers in Fenway Park, it seems to me he's taken this reality to heart. Wherever his life took him—and in his brief time with us, Andre lived more than most ever will—Dubus gratefully received the gifts life offered, working diligently with them for the few years he was granted. And his diligent work is the gift he leaves us, allowing us to appreciate the moments of grace and skill he so freely offers. Remembering the friend of his youth, Jim Valhouli, Dubus puts it this way: "these moments are so pure, they may be sacred; and they are not ephemeral; they seem so, because they exist in Time; but so did my friend Jim Valhouli; a river took his life, but it did not take the life he lived."[3]

Nor has death taken the life Andre Dubus lived and wrote, no matter how much we sorrow at his passing. For his legacy is rich, plentiful, and inspiring—just as he always hoped it would be. As early as 1977 Dubus claimed "the act of writing alone is all I can muster the courage to face in the morning."[4] But what is the source of such courage? In "Marketing" he puts it this way: "I love short stories because I believe they are the way we live. They are what our friends tell us, in their pain and joy, their passion and rage, their yearning and their cry against injustice."[5] Fidelity to life as it is lived has always been the source of Dubus' strength. The passion and rage Dubus explores through the characters in his fiction, their yearnings and cries against injustice, become equally fair ground for him as he tells us his personal stories through his essays.

Imagine a friend telling you a story—yet another in an ongoing series—as you sit down to read Dubus' essays, and you'll be in the proper frame of mind to receive the gifts he's prepared to give. Consider his reflections on telling stories during marriage counseling, "a last act of will to stay married" that usually comes too late.[6] Dubus is quick to clarify the type of storytelling he has in mind, and these stories engage concrete realities of lives lived together, lives that have slowly unraveled. The stories avoid abstractions, firmly rejecting lack of honesty, or lack of commitment.

> [Instead], when we told these stories we discovered the truths that were their essence, that were the very reasons we needed to tell stories; and, like honest fiction writers, we did not know the truth of the stories until we told them. Or, more accurately, until the stories told themselves, took their form and direction from the tactile language of our memory, our pain, and our hope.[7]

As so many times in Dubus' work, life and art intersect here—the honesty of fiction writers that he so admires providing the apt metaphor for the honesty of wives and husbands sharing the deepest truths of their relationships with each other. Such honesty, Dubus suggests, animates the best fiction; such honesty clearly provides the foundation for his personal essays.

The process of engaging such truths, tellingly, is motivated by memory, and seasoned with both pain and hope. Reflecting on this quest for honest human truths in his probing essay "Into the Silence," Dubus arrives at the following insight:

> Short story writers simply do what human beings have always done. They write stories because they have to; because they cannot rest until they have tried as hard as they can to write stories. They cannot rest because they are human, and all of us need to speak into the silence of mortality, to interrupt and ever so briefly stop that quiet flow, and with stories try to understand at least some of it.[8]

Of course, this is what Dubus does in all of his finest stories—whether they take the form of conventional short stories, or rework themselves into one of his intense personal essays. In both cases, he writes because he has to; as a human keenly aware of his mortality, he must speak into the silence.

He speaks into the silence even though he realizes the limited impact such stories might have. Approaching despair at times—"these days I barely have the heart, the will, to do something as insignificant as writing fiction"—his nonfiction essays provide ample room for reflection, for asking tough questions in clear, unadorned prose. Dubus confesses "I have always known that writing fiction had little effect on the world; that if it did, young men would not have gone to war after the *Iliad.*"[9] Yet if it has little effect, what gives a writer the courage or heart to go on? Faced with pain and apathy consuming so much of the world around him, with the random violence and senseless destruction of our day, what gives Dubus his strength? Certainly, he harbors few romantic illusions about his capacity to change the world:

> Only the privileged—those with homes and food and the luxury of time in a home—are touched, moved, and sometimes changed by literature. For the twenty million Americans who are hungry tonight, for the homeless freezing tonight, literature is as useless as a knowledge of astronomy. What do stars look like on a clear cold winter night, when your children are hungry, are daily losing their very health; or when, alone, you look up from a heat grate?[10]

Characteristically, Dubus shares the pity of such a moment with us without lapsing into despair. He concludes the essay noting that his family isn't hungry, isn't homeless, isn't without hope. Still, the retrospective of this narrative allows Dubus the author to realize that the tranquility of home and hearth in the writer's workshop in Iowa also holds the seeds of the collapse of his marriage and family. The hope and promise he believes in then yields the mature understanding that "the only poverty afflicting my wife and me in Iowa City was youth."[11] And the poverty of youth is susceptible to the power of stories; indeed, Dubus constantly searches in the power of stories for something that will ease our passage from youth to maturity.

As in his fiction, in his literary essays Dubus is unapologetically a Catholic writer. He treasures the power of his faith, and, as his literary voice matures, he consistently seeks to translate faith's mysteries into stories that speak to a more universal audience. Indeed, when I've taught both his fiction and nonfiction to undergraduates, I'm often struck by how accessible his work is to students of all beliefs. Consider, for example, Dubus' portrayal of sacraments in his wonderful essay "On Charon's Wharf." "Since we are all terminally ill," the essay begins, "each breath and step and day one closer to the last, I must consider those sacraments which soothe our passage."[12] Although Dubus speaks of a lower case sacrament here, his understanding of sacramental grace clearly owes a debt to his Catholic faith.[13] Like his writing, however, Dubus' faith is moored in the here and now. "My belief in the sacrament of the Eucharist is simple: without touch, God is a monologue, an idea, a philosophy; he must touch and be touched."[14] In its essence, this is the core of Dubus' notion of sacrament—an active and genuine engagement between the world of daily reality and the reality of worldly limits. The idea is as complex as it is central to understanding Dubus' view as a writer, so it's worth exploring in some detail.

> So many of us fail: we divorce wives and husbands, we leave the roofs of our lovers, go once again into the lonely march, mustering our courage with work, friends, half-pleasures which are not whole because they are not shared. Yet I still believe in love's possibility, in its presence on the earth; as I believe I can approach the altar on any morning of any day which may be the last and receive the touch that does not, for me, say: There is no death; but does say: In this instant I recognize, with you, that you must die.[15]

The sacramental vision Dubus espouses is one of touching and being touched. This vision demands engagement, from both the God approached and the human approaching. Recognizing, in the act of Eucharist (which for Catholics actually involves the transubstantiation of bread and wine into Christ's body and blood), a transformation of pain and failure into a redemptive embrace of endless possibility, Dubus takes the ordinary act of sharing a meal—of scrambling eggs—and makes of it something extraordinary, something sacramental.[16] In the inevitable journey toward death, "we are pausing in the march to perform an act together; we are in love; and the meal offered and received is a sacrament which says: I know you will die; I am sharing food with you; it is all I can do, and it is everything."[17] For Dubus, food is sacrament. Love is sacrament. Friendship is sacrament. And perhaps most of all, writing is sacrament—fully recognizing the cosmic futility of the gesture at the very time it asserts, "it is all I can do, and it is everything."

If there is a dominant sensibility in Dubus' essays, then, it is this: the sacrament of writing is all he can hope for, and in that hope is everything. Clearly, this is a sacramental view of life, a life that catches Dubus in every phase rushing toward grace, but one never more clearly expressed than in the years following his tragic accident in July of 1986. One of the real gems in his collection *Broken Vessels* is the very brief essay "Bastille Day." I'm not sure you can tell an entire life story in 300 words, but in this essay Dubus comes close to doing so. In the opening paragraph he narrates the death of his father, the collapse of his first marriage and separation from his four children, then the death of his mother. The next paragraph takes up his service as a marine, the loss through divorce of his next two wives and two more children, and the loss of "my left leg above the knee and most of the functioning of my right one" which required seven weeks of hospitalization and ten operations.[18] How do you follow up two paragraphs that reveal such news? How do you wrap up the essay, and the life, in just one more paragraph? Dubus finds hope in seeing his father "leaving his malignant flesh" and in the very smallness of his own needs, despite being confined to a wheelchair for the remainder of his days. But the clincher is in the final sentence: "Now I see [my father] assaulting with me the gate, the walls, the prison and armory of our flesh: my father in his final and radiant harmony, and I crippled in my chair: mere men, rushing to grace."[19] This rush toward grace, this unrestrained embrace of a sacramental view of life, this assault on the imprisoning walls of our flesh and our mortality mark a transformation of Dubus' spirit as much as they do of his body. Commenting on the essays that rise from the ashes of the accident, Tobias Wolff suggests "they tell of a body irrevocably broken, and the part of a life that depended on that body irrevocably lost, and the struggle of a spirit to build something new."[20] Wolff is a careful reader of Dubus, one who understands the power of stories to help us understand the world around us, but one who also embraces mystery and miracle when appropriate. And that's what he sees finally in Dubus' essays: "He is open to mystery, and of all mysteries the one that interests him most is the human potential for transcendence."[21]

But how do you transcend an accident that cripples you for life? How do you transcend the loss of three wives and six children through divorce? How do you transcend the pain that grips you every day, the fatigue that flattens you, the emotions that paralyze you? In "Lights of the Long Night" Dubus gingerly tries to assemble the disconnected memories from the night of the accident. He remembers the headlights speeding toward him, but not the impact. He remembers the twenty-three-year-old man next to him who died in the crash, and the man's sister whose life he saved. Much of the evening is a blur, but Dubus knows that he pushed the woman out of harm's way, just as he knows "I had chosen to stand there, rather than leap toward the guard rail."[22] Finally, he knows that both the woman and their doctor believe Dubus saved the woman's life that night. And he knows he survived. "I am forever a cripple, but I am alive, and I am a father and a husband, and in 1987 I am sitting in the sunlight of June and writing this."[23] Can nobility transcend pain? Can merely surviving? Or does it take children and sunlight and writing to inspire lasting transcendence?

In another essay, "Sketches at Home," Dubus reviews the same memories. As he's discussing the evening with his doctor, and thanking him for saving his life, Dubus explains to the doctor "why I had wanted to be the one who had saved the woman: because now that I was certain, I could never be angry at myself for stopping and going out on the highway to them, and their car."[24] Transforming anger into acceptance, rage at the injustice of life into peace in its sunlight, Dubus often turns to writing personal essays as a way of understanding the profound physical, emotional, and spiritual transformations life thrusts upon him. The process of understanding these changes is long and arduous, the moments of peace or insight hard-won. One year after the accident, Dubus is able to forgive the driver who hit him. Twenty-two months later, he begins to recognize kindred spirits in soldiers wounded or maimed by war, and he comes to realize that "even war is forgivable, as all human actions can be, ought to be." Coming to terms with what can and ought to be forgiven slowly emerges as a defining theme in the more recent essays Dubus has written, and although clearly related to the sacramental vision he brings to the world, such forgiveness always comes with a price. In war, for example,

> After the dead are buried, and the maimed have left the hospitals and started their new lives, after the physical pain of grief has become with time, a permanent wound in the soul, a sorrow that will last as long as the body does, after the horrors become nightmares and sudden daylight memories, then comes the transcendent and common bond of human suffering, and with that comes forgiveness, and with forgiveness comes love . . . [25]

Coming to terms with the transcendent and common bond of suffering is the first, absolutely necessary, step in transforming pain with forgiveness.

For Dubus, the path parallels that of his sacramental understanding of our mortality. When we feed one another, fully cognizant of our mortality—knowing it is all we can do, and yet that it is everything—we take the risk of loving one another. Such love implies a headlong rush toward grace, a grace that passes all human understanding, yet one capable of transforming human suffering into forgiveness and love. This is the idea that gives Dubus the title for his first collection of essays, the recognition prompted by the Book of Jeremiah and his physical therapist, Mrs. T. As Mrs. T translates: "*It's in Jeremiah . . . the potter is making a pot and it cracks. So he smashes it, and makes a new vessel. You can't make a new vessel out of a broken one. It's time to find the real you.*"[26] And that, of course, is what Dubus has been about throughout his collection of essays in *Broken Vessels*. Carefully turning the pieces of his past life over in his hands, delicately measuring each for its fit in his post-accident, radically transformed life, Dubus has gradually been collecting the shards of his previous life so that he can find his new self. Memory may indeed be responsible for his identity, but he must search for new connections between past and present if he's ever going to make sense of his surroundings. Witness first to death, then to an altered but inspired life, Dubus discovers a place to meditate upon the world around him—and so he begins seeing the world from his movable chair.

His final collection of essays, *Meditations from a Movable Chair,* consistently arcs toward forgiveness and acceptance, a forgiveness and acceptance forged in the smithy of his crippled life, one willing to ask difficult questions of himself, and of his readers. In his essay "Song of Pity," for example, he describes an early encounter with a friend in a wheelchair during his time as a graduate student in the writing program at the University of Iowa. "My friend was very skillful in his wheelchair, and I lacked imagination. Or I lacked the compassion and courage to imagine someone else's suffering."[27] Beyond the bounty memory offers a writer, how much imagination is necessary to compose a good story? And in life, beyond the limits of memory, how much imagination—born of courage and compassion—must we exercise in order to apprehend, and perhaps transform, the suffering of the world around us? As Dubus meditates from his chair in the final years of his life, he shares with us a voice of experience, but his experience is that of personal memory sustained by the transforming power of imagination. The song he sings of pity isn't an appeal for us to pity *him* but rather a song he knows *we* need to hear.

> I sing for those who cannot. To view human suffering as an abstraction, as a statement about how plucky we all are, is to blow air through brass while the boys and girls march in parade off to war. Seeing the flesh as only a challenge to the spirit is as false as seeing the spirit as only a challenge to the flesh. On the planet are people with whole and strong bodies, whose wounded spirits need the constant help that the quadriplegic needs for his body.[28]

And so Dubus sings to us and for us, inviting us to join in the song. Witness to both grief and prayer, he fights for balance in his life—a daily struggle with formidable forces that seek to unsettle him.

Significantly, his struggle to find peace and acceptance is also a struggle to find a story he can live with. "Every day I long for what I used to do: standing, walking, going on long conditioning walks."[29] How do you compensate for the loss of such basic joys? How do you find peace—or make peace—in a world filled with sorrow and loss? "Each day," Dubus claims, "is a struggle against sorrow, with every physical action in the empty house showing me again and again what I have lost. I cannot win this struggle alone."[30] Yet he is profoundly alone in the years following his accident, his third marriage ending a year after the accident, his two young daughters living with their mother. He feels the loss acutely, the brokenness of his body mirroring his shattered spirit.

In part, Dubus finds peace in the very act of writing. Reflecting on his friend, Richard Yates, Dubus imagines Yates "bringing your great heart and your pure writer's conscience to the desk . . . morning after morning."[31] Such imagination gives Dubus hope because "you inspired me, you gave me courage, taking your morning stand against your flesh and circumstance, writing prose that was a blade, a flame, a cloud, a breath."[32] Dubus too takes his morning stand against flesh and circumstance, finding courage and inspiration in the very sacrament of writing. As we noted in *Broken Vessels*, Dubus genuinely believes in the transformative power of stories—a power anchored in "stories about real people," in "words and images" that can literally change the world we live in.

His experience as a volunteer tutor with high school girls struggling to put their lives back together underscores this belief. Discussing Hemingway's "In Another Country" with these girls, Dubus experiences his own moment of epiphany.

> Then, because of my own five years of agony, of sleeping at night and in my dreams walking on two legs, then waking each morning to being crippled, of praying and willing myself out of bed to confront the day, of having to learn a new way to live after living nearly fifty years with a whole body—then, because of all this, I saw something I had never seen in the story . . . and with passion and joy I looked up from the book, looked at the girls' faces, and said: "This story is about healing too."[33]

His ability to discover healing in a story he had long believed was about war, or about the futility of cures, or about the spiritual aging war can cause, or about inconsolable loss, reveals the healing he experiences through stories. But this moment of insight isn't a solitary one. It's an act of community, one that bridges the gap between the stories we read and the stories we live. "The girls watched me," Dubus continues, "nodding their heads, those girls who had suffered and still suffered; but for now, on this Monday night, they sat on my couch, and happily watched me discover a truth; or watched a truth discover me, when I was ready for it."[34] So much of the collection *Meditations from a Movable Chair* is about the saving power of stories and the truths that discover us. In the mature vision of this collection, Dubus relates again and again his readiness to accept the truths offered through stories—both the stories he reads and the stories he lives.

Allowing truth to discover us is harder than it sounds, of course. The opening essay of this collection, "About Kathryn," which describes the rape of Dubus' sister and her attempts to come to terms with it, fronts the gritty reality associated with this process of discovery. "Now I think of her praying for the man who raped her; saying she would have killed him if he had raped her daughter; praying for him; wanting him castrated; praying for him; calling him a jerk."[35] For both Kathryn and Andre, the transcendent truth of forgiveness oscillates with the experienced truth of violation and hate. Finding a place for the truth of forgiveness in the context of his life—which was punctuated for over 30 years with a need to stand and fight injustice whenever he encountered it—is particularly challenging for Andre. But it's hard work he's willing to undertake because of his sister's example, because of the power of her story. "He is gone from her flesh, and she is cleansing her soul; she prays so she can forgive him. It is hard work and will take a long time."[36] With some difficulty, I can follow Dubus up to this point. I know it will be hard work and will take a long time. For me, indeed, it might take an eternity. So I struggle with the truth that finds him in the next sentence: "But one bright day her anger and hatred will burn to white ash, and she will forgive him, the rape will finally end, and the man will be truly gone, to wander in her past."[37] I struggle to imagine forgiveness for a man who had raped my sister, my wife, or my daughter. Of course, Dubus also struggles with such forgiveness, foreshadowing the ultimate quest of his collection of essays. He seeks to open himself to the truths stories will offer—no matter how challenging or problematic—whenever they are willing to offer them. Some he will find in the stories of others; most will emerge from the stories he tells in order to live.

Fully recognizing that he cannot win his daily struggle with sorrow alone, Dubus reaches out to the world of stories, just as he reaches out to his friends and family. Few forces are more powerful aids in his daily struggle than the joy he finds with friends and family. Whether allowing his youngest son to carry him down to the lawn to play ball during a family picnic, or sharing a cigarette with Tim O'Brien at a dinner for writers, Dubus revels in the joy of community. Ten years after his accident, Dubus meets a woman who witnessed his accident from a roadside phone. Both of their lives have gone on, altered for better and worse by that fateful night. The woman now has three sons, the youngest of whom suffers from autism. Piecing together the stories that unite them, and the woman's husband who shared the story over the phone that night, Dubus desperately wants to ask the woman what she saw. But he can't. Instead, the woman goes back inside her home, and a bit later her husband comes out and chats with Dubus. "In his face were the sorrow and tenderness of love as he strongly held his writhing son, looking at the small face that seemed feral in its isolation."[38] Witness to the pain, sorrow, and injustice of life, struggling against its damaging isolation, Dubus finds more solace in the conversation with these people than he does in any facts they reveal about the night of his accident. In a sense, the community of family or friends, and even of chance acquaintances, emerges as the true essence of their individual stories, and becomes the power that saves Dubus.

He hungers for this community in all of his encounters, and finds its most lasting presence in the sacrament of Eucharist, a sacrament that "has sustained my belief in God, who joined us here on earth to eat and drink and be joyful, to love and grieve, to suffer and die."[39] Communion with his God, and with the joy and love or suffering and grief of our human community, give Dubus hope and strength to go on. In the presence of the sacrament of the Eucharist, he discovers "peace of mind came to me and, yes, happiness too, for I was no longer a broken body, alone in my chair. I was me, all of me, in wholeness of spirit."[40] Transforming pain and suffering into wholeness and peace is a central belief Dubus embraces through communion. Tellingly, in the aftermath of his accident, he consistently transforms the sorrow of daily life through communion with others: in his writing, with friends and family, as well as through faith.

Andre Dubus invites us to join him on this daily journey, to commune with him as he rushes toward grace. The formal sacraments of his faith sustain him, just as he invests daily acts of forgiveness, acceptance, or sacrifice with sacramental significance. The sacramental glue that binds all these acts together provides the foundation for the stories he tells, whether in his short stories or novellas, or in his literary nonfiction. In all his work, he stands as a witness to both death and life, to grief and prayers. And it's good for us strangers to join in his witness. When we read his powerful personal essays, he invites us to become "one with all people in pain and joy and passion, one with the physical universe, with Christ, with the timeless dimension of the spirit."[41] His sensitivity to this timeless dimension of the spirit sustains him in his art even as it sustains him in his life. And it is precisely this timeless dimension that allows a crippled man to assault the prison of his flesh even as he rushes to grace.

Graceful and grace-filled, in his best essays Dubus invites his readers to join in such discoveries. The closing section to his moving essay, "Giving Up the Gun," poses such an invitation:

> I have written all of this to try and discover why, sitting in my wheelchair on a train, I gave up my guns. But I do not know. Eight months after that Thanksgiving in Baton Rouge, I was driving home from Boston, armed with a pistol, and I stopped on the highway and got out of my car to help two people who had driven over an abandoned motorcycle. Then a car hit me, and I have been in a wheelchair for over nine years. My body

can no longer do what I want to do, and it cannot protect my two young daughters, and my grandchildren, from perils I used to believe I could save people from. I have not learned the virtue of surrender—which I want—but I have learned the impossibility of avoiding surrender. [42]

Fully aware of the surrenders life forces upon us all, Dubus finds redeeming power in the witness of stories. "Within the realm of human possibility," he says in this essay, "I had done what I could."[43] And that's all we can or should expect of anyone, isn't it? Coming to terms with the realm of human possibility, investing daily in the sacrament of writing, cherishing his majestic rush toward grace, Andre Dubus has certainly done what he could. And we're richer for it.

Notes

[1]Consider Bellah's views in *Habits of the Heart: Individualism and Commitment in American Life*. New York: Harper and Rowe Perennial Library, 1985, 232 (as quoted by Anita Gandolfo, *Testing the Faith: The New Catholic Fiction in America*. New York: Greenwood, 1992, 151). "Thus, in spite of the conservative ambiance of Dubus' fiction, its moral world is the natural extension of contemporary liberal Christianity in which 'community and attachment come not from the demands of a tradition, but from the empathetic sharing of feelings among therapeutically attuned selves.'" Gandolfo then further underscores the unique spin Dubus puts on his inherited faith: "However, the fiction of Andre Dubus and David Plante serves as a significant indicator of the fact that unbridled individualism results in an idiosyncratic Catholicism that has little relation to the Church of history and its tradition" (208). I'm not sure I'd go quite as far as Gandolfo does here—as I do believe Dubus' connection to church history and tradition is somewhat stronger than the case she makes, especially in his literary nonfiction. What's important for our purposes, however, is that the power of community and sharing is unmistakable in both Dubus' fiction and nonfiction.

[2]*Meditations from a Movable Chair: Essays*. New York: Vintage Books, 1999, 76.

[3]77.

[4]"Selling Stories," *Broken Vessels: Essays*. Introduction by Tobias Wolff. Boston: David R. Godine, 1992, 97.

[5]*Broken Vessels*, 104.

[6]92.

[7]92.

[8]92.

[9]87.

[10]87.

[11]89.

[12]77.

[13]I have in mind here the quality that unites a number of American writers whom we might call "Catholic." Ross Labrie, in *The Catholic Imagination in American Literature*. Columbia: U of Missouri P, 1997, focusing on Flannery O'Connor, but with language well suited to Dubus, puts it this way: "What makes O'Connor Catholic is her sacramental view of reality, her sense that experience and time are always edged with spiritual opportunity and with the possibility of religious discovery and decision—no matter how unpromising the circumstances of her characters' lives" (231).

[14]*Broken Vessels*, 77.

[15]78-9.

[16]Although Dubus fleshes out his own notion of sacramental living here, in so doing, he also locates himself firmly within a tradition. For as the Christian poet, Thomas Merton suggests, "the whole world and all the incidents of life tend to be sacraments—signs of God, signs of his love working in the world." (From Thomas Merton, "Poetry and Contemplation: A Reappraisal" in *The Literary Essays of Thomas Merton*, New York: New Directions, 1981, 2.

[17]*Broken Vessels*, 79.

[18]145-6.

[19]146.

[20]xvi.

[21]xv.

[22]130.

[23]131.

[24]134-35.

[25]138.

[26]172.

[27]*Meditations*, 150.

[28]155.

[29]100.

[30]100.

[31]84.

[32]84.

[33]58.

[34]58.

[35]8.

[36]8.

[37]9.

[38]206.

[39]101.

[40]101.

[41]101-02.

[42]192.

[43]192.

Professor and Head of the Department of English and Fine Arts at the United States Air Force Academy, **Thomas G. Bowie, Jr.** is also Managing Editor of *War, Literature & The Arts: An International Journal of the Humanities*. He has written extensively on the literature of the Vietnam War.

Will Hochman

The Ongoing Poetry of Andre Dubus

What does it mean to call a master of prose a poet? J.D. Salinger embodies this question in his Glass stories. Seymour Glass, Salinger's most interesting and most religious character is known as poet, though it's not Glass' one haiku so much as the resonance of the character's soul in the fiction that makes readers believe he's a true poet. Readers may accept Seymour's essential persona as poetic because spiritual and fictive elements create a need to elevate and praise him. A similar effect arises from studying the words and life of Andre Dubus. In his short essay "Bodily Mysteries," Dubus reflects on the Eucharist and declares "since I was a boy, this sacrament has sustained my belief in God, who joined us here on earth to eat and drink and be joyful, to love and grieve, to suffer and die. For most of my life, I have tried to receive the Eucharist daily." Dubus ends this brief, elegant essay about resuming his lifelong religious practice after the accident that confined him to a wheelchair for the rest of his life simply by saying, "I drove my car to church and consumed God." Dubus' deep spirit can be as mundane as starting an engine and driving, and as direct as consuming God. His sense of disjunction, otherness and reversal was certainly keen enough to include and even embrace the irony of being a called a poet as part of the way to remember his literary achievement. After all, Dubus had to believe his best insights would reach beyond the realities of his life but not his words.

The fiction of Andre Dubus had always been infused with the kind of hard luck, disappointment and occasional right moments that were brought strangely into non-fictive focus by the events near the end of the writer's own life. In one of his stories, a character jumps from a sinking ship back into the water in a vain attempt to save the dying captain from sharks. What an eerie precursor for Dubus who was struck by a car after he stopped on the road to help a stranger in distress. In most of Dubus' stories, the characters act through lifetimes of strife and conflict to simply live or maybe glimpse something beyond themselves. As Dubus matured and began writing essays as well as fiction, genre distinctions eroded and the spirit and thrust of his humility progressed. Dubus became the patron saint of dysfunctional American families long before his third marriage ended and he lost the custody of his children.

Read "Miranda Over the Valley" to see how an abortion that was urged by well meaning parents shatters a young girl's entire sense of love. Dubus' ethical world is clear and lacks heavy-handed judgment. The morality in the prose is close to the ground, and rarely if ever spelled out. Instead of diving into polemics, Dubus manages to deal with an argumentatively charged issue by poetically reversing the poles of the conflictual energy. It wasn't a fetus aborted, but love. Dubus practiced creating tough, insightful reversals in most of his work. Read in "Adultery" to see how an unhappily married woman is inspired by her lover's terminal cancer to divorce her husband. Dubus manages in this story to make deceit virtuous by glimpsing poetic truth in sad moments of dying love. Continuing the tradition of "Esthetique du Mal," such poetic reversals often create the author's most enlightening reading effects.

Dubus is a poet in the way he can plant a word in his prose that suddenly scoops up so much resonance and power from the narrative that it often takes the reader by surprise. Read "The Fat Girl." Louise is a young woman who "thought of the accumulated warmth and pelf of her marriage, and how by slimming her body she had bought into the pleasures of the nation." The poetic resonance of sound in these lines is keyed by the sound in "pelf," which leaps out of the sentence and may send some readers directly into their dictionaries. *Webster's Seventh New Collegiate* defines "pelf" simply as "Money: Riches." *The American Heritage College Dictionary* adds to pelf's definition: "Wealth or riches, esp. when dishonestly acquired." And from the very first definition in the *OED*, "pelf" is something tainted and illicit when defined as "property pilfered or stolen, spoil, booty." How pelf is defined—from wealth attained to tainted booty—also parallels the range of meaning the word accumulates in the story's narrative. The poetic reversal of pelf is enacted in how readers can shift from wanting Louise to lose her weight to seeing that the character's weight loss is somehow wrong. Reversals in Dubus' work are complex and usually spiral the plot into the flesh and bones of his characters. There's poetry in this twisting. Consider how powerfully Dubus seems able to inhabit his female characters. Dubus uses his craft to offer surface images that are powerfully revealed to be saying the opposite of what would be anticipated. When readers stay close to Dubus' language they are rewarded with a sense of craft and meaning-making that artfully resonates beyond what narrative events and characters may first indicate.

Part of the poetic element in Dubus' prose is that his ear stays true to the rhythms of everyday talk and experience, while his eye takes us deeply into the souls of his characters and himself. In his essay, "Letter to a Writer's Workshop," Dubus describes thinking about "mindfullness":

> . . . I realized why writing and physical exercise have been so deeply pleasurable for me despite or because of the effort they demand: while doing both of those, if I am concentrating, I am one with the man I normally am not and, achieving or receiving that, I am one with people and truths I will never know when I am my normal self again: driving a car, or watching men throw a baseball, or talking with friends.

This mindfullness is a consciousness of writing for Dubus that is very much centered by his sense of otherness, which perhaps explains his exceptional ability to write from both male and female points of view. John Keat's idea of "negative capability" is another way to phrase Dubus' method of writing himself into "the man I normally am not." Perhaps this otherness also reflects a poetic sense of how something other than ink and words really become the poem. Dubus' empathy for others (in his characters, in his keen sense of audience, and in his life) is advanced by his metaphoric sense that there is always more to be understood than what first meets the eye.

What happens between the lines and in the margins of Dubus' prose is poetry because it leaps from writer to voice to reader in the same ways that direct, real, day-to-day experience helps to explain the mysteries of heart and soul. Dubus does more than report hard, harsh realities; his prose explores the psychological realism of life's struggles, joining reader and text in a focused quest to understand the particular motivation and consequences of the worlds in his words. As in Chekhov's fiction, significance resonates in reader and writer with a variety of possibilities. Dubus' narrative art is secured by his ability to make the best parts of a story not told or shown so much as experienced. Read in "The Lover," where Lee, a middle-aged survivor of three marriages, "learned how quickly love dies when you weren't looking; if you weren't looking." In bed with a new lover, Lee strangely confesses that "Somewhere I missed something. Something my cock can't feel. Even my heart can't feel." The character's emotional emptiness suddenly overtakes readers in the very moment he has found a new lover. Such reversals are stunning in Dubus' work and he maintained the wisdom and craft that lets the ironic angst play out more in readers than "from the writer" or even on the page. He knew that his terse language at his story's most powerful points was an effective way to let the story happen in its most human and real contexts.

In an interview one day before his death, Dubus was asked how he managed to make his dialogue sound so real. He described a sense of craft that depends on a poetic process of purifying language:

> It's probably not real; maybe it tries too hard to be real. You should never write realistic dialogue. We all talk too much. Look at the short stories of Fitzgerald or Hemingway—they write lines that sound like human speech but it's purified. No one says that little. I try to get a poetic rhythm going and I try to write literary dialogue. We're not trying to be real. We're trying to be better than real. We're trying to be true.

Hemingway's influence on Dubus goes into and beyond the clichés of Hemingway's impact on generations of writers. Probably the honesty in Dubus' work is the result of using Hemingway's "crap detector" to screen out all but the truest aspects of story. And possibly Dubus' direct and terse style is the result of Hemingway's distaste for all but the most necessary and influential modifiers. However, as Dubus shows in his essay "A Hemingway Story," he advances beyond the master writer as a masterful and humble reader. Dubus sets up the power of reading's influence on writing by remembering a drink with Ralph Ellison and Kurt Vonnegut. Ellison admitted that he had to read Malraux's *Man's Fate* forty times before starting to write *Invisible Man*. Dubus responded by saying that he's been re-reading Hemingway stories and believed his favorite was "In Another Country." Ellison spontaneously recited the first paragraph of Hemingway's story. This moment in Dubus' essay illustrates Hemingway's impact without needing to explain it. The authors over drinks and words become a metaphor for "The Writer." As Wallace Stevens says in his poem "Metaphors of a Magnifico," "Twenty men crossing a bridge,/ Into a village,/ Are twenty men crossing twenty bridges,/ Into twenty villages,/ Or one man/ Crossing a single bridge into a village." Dubus ends that stunning literary moment and first part of the essay shortly after Ellison speaks Hemingway's first paragraph. As readers read Hemingway in the voice of Ellison and in the prose of Dubus, it's insightful to imagine that Hemingway's first words are meant to be read and spoken like poetry in the combined voice of all writers.

Later in "A Hemingway Story," Dubus says "A story can always break into pieces while it sits inside a book on a shelf; and, decades after we have read it even twenty times, it can open us up, by cut or caress, to a new truth." He is setting up his own epiphany about interpreting the Hemingway story anew because of his crippling accident. Dubus is also demonstrating how polysemy makes a story work poetically. The possibility of multiple meanings in the same fictional text is the same literary phenomenon that enables metaphors in poetry to render new meanings over time and in different readers. The point of "A Hemingway Story," like the poetry in Dubus' prose, is centered by more than reading a story and "getting it"—it's about readers living the story and getting it to a point where the narrative lives more honestly as ongoing possibility.

Andre Dubus will take his place among the great short story writers of our time. He never made enough from teaching or writing to reward his efforts justly, but for Dubus, advancing his principles and craft may have always been the only possible profit from his work. In "A Salute to Mister Yates," Dubus admires Richard Yates, who, despite living most of his life in poverty, was a great writer because he only wanted and valued readers. It takes one to know one! In *Broken Vessels*, Dubus wrote

> The act of writing alone is all I can muster the courage to face in the morning; if my livelihood and the expectations of publishers depended on it, I doubt that I could do it at all. So, like the poets, short story writers live in a safer world. There is no one to sell out to, there is no one to hurry a manuscript for; our only debt is to ourselves, and to those stories that speak to us from wherever they live until we write them.

When Dubus died on February 24, 1999, he began another poetic reversal. His death will allow his work and reputation to grow larger in the hearts and minds of his readers. Many of us admire the man a great deal, but the larger respect and love that Dubus' future readers will create is predictable. The rich seeds of life left behind in the writer's words resonate and echo honesty like our best poems do. Beyond genre, Dubus' mastery of truth-telling so clearly shows how he crafted language to create life that calling it poetry only begins to respect this writer's craft. Generous to the word, Dubus lived with his eternal questioning and difficult sense of honesty while constantly keeping his eye on what helps others.

Will Hochman is co-editor of *Letters to J.D. Salinger* (University of Wisconsin Press). His creative writing and criticism have appeared most recently in the *North American Review, Connecticut Review, Small Press Review,* and *The Missouri Review.* Hochman is the Poetry Editor of *War, Literature & the Arts: An International Journal of the Humanities* and the Reviews Editor of *Academic Writing.*

Ross Gresham

The Interviews

Andre Dubus gave twenty or more interviews between 1981 and his death in 1999. Reading them, one gets several different pictures of the man. I'd like to begin with the simplest of these, because it's as a caricature that I first encountered him.

The Caricature

Unlike many others writing in this collection, I never met Andre Dubus. I came to know him as we all must now, through his writings of course, but in my case first through the ancillary materials: these interviews, and also the stories I heard about him—stories like those in this collection— and the pictures on the back covers of his books. In most of the pictures he has chosen not to dress up. There's no desk, no bookcases behind him, and sometimes he wears a blue-collar hat. A big man, with a beard.

My dad got an M.F.A. at Iowa. He was there when Kurt Vonnegut asked the class if anyone had a novel. A bearded guy down front said he did but that it wasn't any good. Vonnegut said he better take a look anyway. Later in the year Vonnegut brought in the acceptance letter and read it to the class. The bearded guy was Dubus.

At the time, while he was teaching in the Writers' Workshop, Vonnegut was taking graduate English classes (including Old English) toward a Ph.D. so he could get a real teaching job. I mention this because it shows how much college English departments have changed since my dad got his M.F.A. in the late 1960's. These days a writer of Vonnegut's caliber would count on getting a job just by the strength of his writing. And I mention all this because I came to know Dubus through the writer-in-the-academy culture as it grew and flourished between now and then.

I went to writing school in the South in the early nineties. Dubus was one of the writers to read, then, but more importantly he was one of the writers to be like. That is why the Dubus pictures are important: no bookshelves in the background, the blue-collar hat, no tie. Writers, whether visiting or on staff, behaved differently from the rest of the English faculty. The caricature is pretty easy to draw: "Shit, I lost my plane ticket! Who the fuck are all these eggheads? Reading *Moby Dick* makes my brain hurt! Where's the bar? Honey, to be a writer you've got feel it here, here, here in your heart. Feel that?"[1] Let me repeat that I never met Andre Dubus. I heard a few wild visiting-writers stories about him, I saw a few dust-jacket photos, and I read the cool Vintage Contemporaries edition of his stories. He and a dozen other contemporary writers, with their booze and antics, formed an appealing (and no doubt unrealistic, unfair) amalgam. The other students and I were fascinated by the tales; we passed them around third-hand; we talked about the adventures as much as the work. We wanted to write, but as much as that, I'm convinced, most of us wanted to be The Writer.

Which as I say is an unfair caricature. But there are good reasons for such a character to have developed (especially, as I've said, since the late 60's) and for it to have so much appeal—the cartoon Dubus, but also the cartoon versions of Raymond Carver, Richard Ford, Barry Hannah, and the others. And that is the ease and expertise with which a practicing writer, with which Dubus, talks about books and writing. Writers have become more important in English departments as English department scholarship has drifted away from judgment and plain speaking. As though from some sort of science envy, most literary scholarship and most English professors don't use the same language as the works they're examining. They are also embarrassed to make value judgments about literature. Isn't it strange that English professors don't generally write book reviews? Shouldn't they best be able to compare the latest Updike to his others? No, for this job we call upon practicing writers. Into the sometimes bloodless world of the academy, it's easy to drop like a bomb. Dubus:

> The last time I was teaching *Dubliners*, I threw the book against the ceiling and said I would never teach that book again. You see, Joyce likes only a few people, the little boy in "Araby" and then two or three sisters in various stories. The rest of the book is written with scorn, even though it is probably the most

beautifully crafted book of stories in the world. There is no love, no heart.... As you see, I can't stand Joyce. I have not read anything of his for a long time. I think he was a self-absorbed son of a bitch.[2]

Dubus is right about *Dubliners*. But were he to say this at a Joyce conference, there would be a few coughs, a few embarrassed condescending smiles, before those present would turn to the matter at hand, new developments in the application of Historical Energy theory to the letters written by Joyce's brother to a little known book collector of the time. It wouldn't be that Dubus' observations were too obvious; it's that Joyce is a canonized master and scholars would see their job now as accumulating interpretations of the work. There are plenty of reasons, good and bad, why English scholarship shies away from plain statement and aesthetic judgment, but in doing so scholars leave the heart of the reading experience, the important part, to someone else. In many English departments, writers have filled the gap.

In his interviews, like many writers, Dubus makes pronouncements on literature that one once might have expected a professor to make: Chekhov is the master. Camus's fiction is weak because "you can see an idea being worked out...."[3] Sartre's fiction is weak for the same reason.[4] "Updike writes like a woman" (this meant as a compliment).[5]

Dubus' opinions are bluntly stated: "If Nabokov's characters are galley slaves, I might understand why [...] while having the flu in Iowa years ago, I was reading Lolita, getting a hard-on, then I got well, and never remembered to pick it up again. I do not think any good writer has characters who are galley slaves."[6] While he talks with great confidence, he doesn't pretend authority, or that he has read everything, which allows him more latitude than most of us would normally be comfortable giving: "...another time it was South African writers, but I couldn't find many in those days. Nadine Gordimer and Andre Brink I could find without a problem. I couldn't find many blacks, and the blacks I was able to find were not very good. I guess it was because they hadn't been able to read much."[7] Like some of the writers he's been linked with— Tobias Wolff, Raymond Carver—he doesn't think much of postmodern innovation (work by writers like John Barth, William Gass, Robert Coover): "it's like raw oysters and fried brains; you can't call a man an asshole for not liking it."[8]

Dubus taught in an English department for 18 years, so he's aware of this philosophical split that has developed in some English departments. He knows which side he's on: "You've got to unteach [students] many things. I think a lot of English teachers don't teach well. They teach literature as if it's a thing to acquire. They go a little crazy symbol-hunting."[9] In more than one place he's skeptical of the idea of literature divided into historical lines, or schools, or periods: "I think it is a game teachers play so they can have a package. 'In this six weeks we'll cover this line of writers,' and that takes care of that, as though they are studying evolution. I don't think it's that simple."[10] It's a subject Dubus can get passionate about: "I asked my friend the poet Kenneth F. Rosen why do so many teachers present literature as something you understand, package, and put away? He said because they treat it like an acquisition, and like all people who devote their lives to acquisition, they're cowards."[11]

The Practicing Writer

Interviewers frequently ask Dubus questions about how his writing actually gets done. In several interviews he talks about using Hemingway's trick of stopping mid-sentence to leave something to begin with the next day.[12] Other interesting notes: while editing, Dubus read his stories into a tape recorder.[13] Early in his career he would write multiple drafts. Then in about 1986, with the story "Anna," he began instead writing fewer drafts more carefully, a stylistic shift he calls horizontal to vertical: "I went very slowly, and as a result, the story was finished more quickly."[14]

It's also common in the interviews for Dubus to comment on the current state of publications for short fiction. He generally likes literary quarterlies, who accept or reject a story but rarely ask the writer for changes. He is hard on most of the glossies, especially *The New Yorker*, which he calls, "one of the worst influences on young writers in America." He doesn't like the way the magazine uses its great clout to change writers' stories: "…they don't care whether they take the guts out of a story or change the voice of it. Now I'm always grateful when the characters fuck in my stories because it puts me beyond them."[15]

The Man (and the Catholic)

Interviews, I have discovered, are a very repetitive form. Most of the shorter interviews with Andre Dubus are informal, touch-the-writer pieces, two-page magazine spreads in which the interviewer first narrates the colorful elements of Dubus' life (Southern-Cajun, Marine, Catholic, and, later, heroic victim of an accident), then laces in a few choice quotations culled from what must have been a much longer conversation. These interviews serve their purpose, letting us meet the famous man, but they tend to draw the simpler caricature I describe above.

One reason we read interviews with famous people is to have our stereotypes reinforced. We expect Hollywood stars to be interviewed poolside, and we expect writers to come across as wild men who don't count beer as drinking, and who lose pieces of their rental tuxedo the night they accept the Pulitzer Prize. That's what we pay our money for— we read interviews with writers partly to rub up against the Promethean spark. But we also read them for what seems to me a better reason: something in the work makes the writer sound like someone whose company we would enjoy, who sees the world as we do or at least in a way interesting to us. An interview allows us to meet a fiction writer without the fictional masks. Late in his life Dubus published two collections of essays, and these scoop some of what I would be looking for in a candid interview—if not the material, then the voice, the sense of unmediated connection.[16] But read all the interviews with Dubus that you can get your hands on, and you can still flesh him out.

To take a personal example, I came to understand Dubus' Catholicism. I held off reading Dubus for a long time because he is so regularly referred to as a Catholic writer. No doubt many writers have religious feeling, but to identify yourself as a religious writer, to me, sets up certain expectations, and all of them are bad. There are plenty of singers out there, many of them Christians, but if one steps up to the microphone and identifies herself as a Christian singer, I'm going to get my jacket. From a writer who identifies himself as a religious writer, I expect a simplified worldview, where the author's sympathies for characters correspond to these characters' beliefs or lack thereof as though they wore badges or black and white cowboy hats. Worse, I expect I might find the plot manipulated to demonstrate religious platitudes: meek characters inheriting the earth by their goodness and charity...claymation stuff. Or maybe just as bad—and a chief concern when I hear specifically of Catholicism—I expect I might start to trip over a system of symbols I know and care nothing about.

Yet the immediate salient feature of Andre Dubus' fiction, and then upon further consideration the strongest element, the thing that may make his work timeless, is the lack of easy formulations in his characters. This is surprising in any author, and sometimes unsettling. In "The Pretty Girl," the leading man, Ray, rapes his ex-wife at knife point. The scene is given in brutal detail. Yet the fabric of the story doesn't change at all for it. Ray is still the lead character, his justification for the rape unexpected and uncomfortably spiritual: "I was taking back my wife for a while; and taking back, for a while anyway, some of what she took from me. That is what it felt like: I went to her place torn and came out mended. Then she was torn, so I was back in her life for a while." No one revenges Polly, or even makes too much of an effort to try, and gradually the story forgets the crime. Later Ray makes another late-night visit, with ambiguous motives, and Polly shoots him dead. The story closes with a passage from the point of view of Ray's brother, who mourns his death and despises Polly.

Rape, or other violence against the helpless (children, animals), means only one thing in modern narrative—the perpetrator is the villain, the blocking figure, etc. After the rape scene, the hero will begin his vendetta. In "The Pretty Girl," Ray is not presented as a hero or a villain, neither a figure who needs to triumph nor a figure who needs to be defeated. Dubus gives Ray his justifications, which he does not hold up as being obviously flawed, just as he gives Polly and the grieving brother their reasons for doing things, all of them unchallenged in the world of the story. More than any writer I can think of, Dubus avoids casting his characters in roles. This may be most striking when the characters are criminals (the sympathetic robbers in "Anna," or the murdering boy in "Townies"). But he does the same in the rest of his work. In "The Pitcher," a minor league pitcher finds out that his wife has been unfaithful and is leaving him for a dentist; he goes off to pitch a baseball game and by the end of it he both forgives her and comes to pity her. There are none of the conventional histrionics—shouting, gun threats, hatred. In *Voices from the Moon*, a young woman plans to marry the father of her ex-husband. The son and father have some heated conversations, but in the end, in this family where there is every chance for bitterness, hatred, lasting dysfunction, cruel words, and revenge, there is peace. When you read *Voices from the Moon*, it is at once alien and familiar—these characters are not like characters in stories; they are familiar, though, as people, with the sort of heightened maturity that prevents the real world from dissolving into gunplay at every adulterous affair. The world of this novella acknowledges that though there is pain and offense, there can be, mitigating these, real familial love.

The interviews reconcile this sensitive, realistic characterization with Dubus' religion. It's not that his devotion has been exaggerated. He seems as religious as anyone I have come across. He went to Catholic healing services: "There were three or four stations, people lining up, laying on of hands...."[17] He believed God had an actual physical presence in the world: "It's said the Virgin Mary told those children she's been appearing to in Yugoslavia that when you pray for someone an angel sits on that person's shoulder. Isn't that beautiful? I have no trouble believing that, quite literally."[18] Yet the interviews reveal that we are not seeing some sort of Christian forgiveness enacted on pitiful characters. In the interviews, Dubus the man clearly does empathize with his characters, even with Ray: "But she put him through so much pain that he cannot bear imagining her walking around that same moment breathing a portion of the same air he's breathing. So when he rapes her, he feels as though something in him has returned which was taken away, something was healed."[19] Rather than judge by religious standards, Dubus withholds judgment, in a way he would characterize as godlike:

> It seems to me that when you are writing and when you are reading somebody who is really superb, you become like God, with that kind of compassion and love. You can become the character you are reading about and understand why he or she does everything he does, love that person, and then you close the book and you can return to the world of judgments and many times that world of judgments is a good place to return to.[20]

In the interviews in which Dubus discusses his stories, he makes it clear that once he knows the characters he just follows along as they act as they must. He talks as though he can't control their actions, and is even saddened by things they end up doing. In several interviews he talks about trying to rewrite "Miranda Over the Valley" because Miranda kept disappointing him with how she was behaving: "I wrote the ending over several times because she was so hard at the end and I didn't want her to be so hard. I kept writing that last scene over and over, but Miranda remained hard."[21] He's disappointed by the behavior of the lead character at the end of *The Lieutenant*: "I remember being very sad and telling my wife, 'Tierney just copped out.'"[22] He is disappointed with Polly when she shoots Ray ("The Pretty Girl," mentioned above).[23]

Andre Dubus on His Stories

It may be interesting to learn how Dubus feels about Miranda at the end of "Miranda Over the Valley," but you run the risk of spoiling the story. If we find out what an author was trying to say, or thinks was said, then our interest in reading the story comes not from standard freshness of encountering and interpreting a world but from the more academic pleasure of seeing whether an author successfully accomplished what he set out to do. It is difficult to discover your own reading of a story when you know the author's intent.[24] Dubus himself seems to realize this risk. Talking about Flannery O'Connor he said, "I wish I had never read that quote of hers where she said that she writes about sacraments that nobody believes in. Every time I read her stories I look for the sacraments and get lost in the story."[25]

All the long interviews, especially the one with Kennedy, quote Dubus stating his intent in writing various stories and his own feelings toward them. These commentaries are disappointing, as any such summaries must be. Dubus' thick, complicated characters have their problems explained. Still, the statements are obviously of some value if you care to go farther into Dubus' head during the process of composition, farther than the stories themselves allow.

Notes

[1]This picture is deliberately cartoonish. However, the bar line is taken from an entertaining account of Dubus doing a visiting writer workshop at the University of Indiana (in Schildhouse: "Our Dinners with Andre"). The "Interview with Andre Dubus" in /excerpt/ has a similar feel.

[2]Samway, *Xavier Review*, 3.
[3]Hayes 24.
[4]Kennedy 91.
[5]Levasseur and Rabalais 56.
[6]Kennedy 91.
[7]Levasseur and Rabalais 47.
[8]Kennedy 89.
[9]Dahlin 56.
[10]Kennedy 93.
[11]Hathaway 96.
[12]Todd 100.

[13]Levasseur and Rabalais 44, among other places.

[14]*Contemporary Authors Online*. Also Todd 98, Smolens 3, etc.

[15]Holmes 8.

[16]Most of the questions in one of his good late interviews (Wachtel) ask him to comment on things he's said in his essays. Most of the time Dubus clarifies rather than adds.

[17]Todd 106.

[18]Lyons and Oliver, "Passion is Better," 158.

[19]Kennedy 110; similar feelings for Anna, are, among other places, in *Contemporary Authors Online* or the "Interview with Andre Dubus" in */excerpt/*.

[20]Kennedy 122.

[2] Samway, *Xavier Review*, 10. Todd 101. Levasseur and Rabalais 42.

[22]Samway, *Xavier Review*, 13.

[23]Kennedy 91. Here he contrasts this way of thinking of character with the Nabokov "galley slave" method.

[24]A fine example of the distance between academic theory (author is dead, unimportant to reading, etc.) and actual process of reading.

[25]Samway, *America*, 300.

Dubus Interviews

"A Conversation with Andre Dubus." *Image* 3 (Spring 1993): 40+.

Contemporary Authors Online. "Interview." 10 May 1985. Gale Group, 2000.

Dahlin, R. "Interview with Andre Dubus." *Publisher's Weekly* 12 Oct. 1984: 56-57.

Hathaway, Dev. "A Conversation with Andre Dubus." *Black Warrior Review* 9.2 (Spring 1983): 86-103.

Hayes, Larry. "Interview: Andre Dubus." *AEGIS* 9.1 (Spring 1981): 17-26.

Holmes, Jon. "With Andre Dubus." *Boston Review* 9.4 (Jul.-Aug. 1984): 7-8.

"Interview with Andre Dubus." *Art & Soul*. 23 Feb. 1999. <http://www.Baylor.edu/~Rel_Lit/dubus.html>.

"Interview with Andre Dubus." */excerpt/*. <http://www.english.swt.edu/excerpt.dir/excerpt1.dir/dubus1.htm>.

Kennedy, Thomas E. "Raw Oysters, Fried Brains, the Leap of the Heart: An Interview with Andre Dubus." *Delta* 24 (Feb. 1987): 21-77.

Levasseur, Jennifer and Kevin Rabalais. "Interview." *Glimmer Train Stories* 31 (Summer 1999): 39-59.

Lyons, Bonnie and Bill Oliver. "Andre Dubus: An Interview." *Crazyhorse* 44 (Spring 1993): 90-101.

—. "Passion is Better." In *Passion and Craft: Conversations with Notable Writers*. Urbana: U of Illinois Press, 1998: 145-58.

McCarthy, Tim. "Andre Dubus' knuckler keeps him in the game." *The National Catholic Reporter* 13 Jul. 1990.

Nathan, Robert. "Interview with Andre Dubus." *Bookletter* 3.12 (14 Feb. 1987): 14-15.

Read, Mimi. "Interview with Andre Dubus." *Sunday Times Picayune Dixie Roto Magazine*, Summer 1984.

Samway, Patrick. "An Interview with Andre Dubus." *America* 14 Nov. 1987: 300-301.

—. "Interview with Andre Dubus." *Xavier Review* 8.1-2 (Spring-Fall 1998): 1-15.

Schildhouse, Amy. "Our Dinners with Andre." *Indiana Review* 10.1/2 (1987): 9-20.

Smolens, John. "An Interview with Andre Dubus." *AWP Chronicle* 29.1 (Sept. 1996): 1-6.

Todd, David Yandell. "An Interview with Andre Dubus." *Yale Review* 86.3 (Jul. 1998): 89-110.

Wachtel, Eleanor. "Andre Dubus." In *Writers & Company*. San Diego: Harvest, 1993. 125-137.

Ross Gresham is Assistant Professor of English at the United States Air Force Academy.

9 June 1992

...hunger and lips when she smiled.

To Robert's left, while he ate, was the living room, and to his rear the kitchen. Behind Lydia was a very wide window the wall was glass and saw a large window, and the wide deep and deep back lawn ending at woods. They had four acres with many trees and they could not see their neighbors' houses; even now, in winter, there were enough evergreens so all the earth they saw from the house was their own. Before dinner Lydia drew drew the curtains at her back; she felt exposed through the glass. On Robert's second night at home

"The Colonel's Wife"
2nd draft

Robert E. Skinner

A Descriptive Bibliography

Although Andre Dubus left no formal memoir, his stories and essays, read first to last, provide as accurate a record of his moral and intellectual growth as any autobiography. His indelible portraits of ordinary men and women struggling to live life honorably, to find love and emotional security, sometimes failing because of an inability to resist their baser instincts, mirror his own struggles to be a good husband, father, friend, and writer. His essays, in particular, tell us the kind of man he was at each stage, and also provide a kind of picaresque story of his genesis and growth as a writer and as a man.

In one of his earliest occasions in print, we find an earnest (and somewhat priggish) youngster accusing the owners of the open-air drive-in theaters in his hometown of trying to wreck the morals of impressionable youth with salacious advertising and immoral movies. Toward the end, he's a man, in poor health no longer young, trying to come to terms with pain and failure as he seeks beauty and fulfillment in the time he has left to live.

In between we find what is perhaps the most interesting part of his story—why he deliberately chose the relatively penurious life of teacher and short fiction writer over the possible wealth and fame he might have won as a novelist. In a 1977 essay he wrote, "I have never envied writers who make a lot of money, because the casual combination of money and writing frightens me. The act of writing alone is all I can muster the courage to face in the morning."[1]

He explains that after spending many years trying to write a story that would make it into *Esquire*, he eventually decided "It would be nice to appear in *Esquire*, but nice finally isn't very much, and one can live peacefully without it."[2] This was the beginning of his recognition that the price of making it into the high-paying slick magazines might well be the sacrifice of his artistic vision.

He gets to the crux of the matter when he confronts the issue of losing the rights to his words when a lot of money has been paid for them. As a budding writer, he allowed three words ("horny," "brown-nose," and "diaphragm") to be excised from his first story published in *The New Yorker* in 1967. He was paid the then astronomical sum of $2,250 for it, feeling "excited, but scared too, and I should have been."[3]

Dubus' epiphany, if it can be called that, occurred when, at mid-career, he sold a story to *Penthouse*. He was not afforded the opportunity to see the galleys, and when the story finally appeared in print, he found that "in a sixteen-page manuscript, someone had made eighty-five changes."[4] His volatile reaction lost him a subsequent sale to *Penthouse*, but he had learned something from the experience. It is noteworthy that a story with the same title as the bowdlerized *Penthouse* story appears in one of his anthologies, but the prior publication in *Penthouse* is not noted. This would apparently happen again, until he virtually forsook the slick magazines for the artistic freedom accorded to him in the literary quarterlies. For Dubus, his words held more value than the money he might be paid for them.

He expanded on this theme in a subsequent *Boston Magazine* essay in February 1978. He opens the essay by explaining that he prefers short stories because "I believe they are the way we live."[5] He goes on to relate the odyssey that eventually led to his ultimate goal in those days—a published book of his own stories.

He faced a considerable obstacle in this quest. The large trade presses avoid collections of stories because of a widely held belief that story collections make no money. Every publisher Dubus contacted would publish his collection of stories only if he would promise to produce a novel for them. That Dubus didn't want to write a novel or to even make any money found no sympathy or understanding.[6]

Eventually, Dubus, acting on advice, secured a literary agent, and the agent helped Dubus realize his eighteen-year dream by placing that first collection with David Godine in Boston. Godine's willingness to publish story collections with no strings attached earned him Dubus' unflinching loyalty—a loyalty that persisted until Dubus' death in 1999.

Although few writers actually make much money from their work, fewer yet approach the craft without at least some hope that they'll achieve both critical and financial success. Dubus' stubborn belief that the inviolability of his words was more important than financial gain is what makes him both quixotic and heroic, and perhaps insures that his work will always be alive in any discussion of the modern American short story.

To embark on the creation of a literary bibliography is, itself, somewhat quixotic, if for no other reason than the fact that the discipline of creative writing is so poorly cataloged. Even when there existed a short story index in print, many literary quarterlies and magazines were not comprehensively surveyed by its editors. The same can be said for creative nonfiction. What bibliography exists has sometimes been inaccurate, or has perpetuated the inaccuracies of earlier bibliographers and critics.

Like most writers, Dubus published wherever he could in the beginning, but even as he became established and a regular contributor to more important publications, he still occasionally published in magazines that were relatively obscure. A few are not possible to identify or locate even using such sophisticated electronic tools as the World Wide Web and OCLC.

When electronic resources proved unhelpful, I often resorted to calling the editorial offices of the magazines or newspapers in question. All but a few responded in a helpful and generous fashion, although I discovered that some magazines of considerable longevity had no internal index or office connection to draw upon for information about previous contributors.

Every effort was made to completely identify the original text in the original organ, even if Dubus did not acknowledge the appearance as his work. When that was not possible, I have provided as much information as I was able to glean from my research, and from those people who assisted me.

The bibliography is composed of four sections: 1) First Periodical Fiction Appearances, 2) Story Collections and other Books, 3) First Periodical Nonfiction Appearances, and 4) Essay Collections.

Section 1 includes a full citation for the original magazine appearance. A code number will refer the user to each of Dubus' collections in which the story later appeared. Citations are also included to lead the user to anthologies that reprint the story.

Section 2 includes a citation for each of Dubus' books, and a list of citation code numbers to indicate which of the stories in Section 1 appeared in each book. Also included are limited editions which reprint individual Dubus stories.

Section 3 includes first periodical appearances for each of Dubus' essays, with code numbers indicating in which of Dubus' two collections individual essays have been included. Citations appear for anthologies in which individual essays have been reprinted.

Section 4 provides bibliographic information for Dubus' two collections of essays, with code numbers to indicate which of the essays in Section 3 are collected.

While every effort was made to precisely identify each item described, it is a rare bibliography that makes it to print completely error-free. Although I contacted many people in my quest to track down and identify everything Dubus ever published, in the end I must bear the responsibility for all mistakes and omissions discovered by subsequent readers.

Section 1

Fiction: First Periodical Appearances

1950s

S-1 "Vendetta." *The Contraband* 19 No. 2 (April 1, 1958): 2, 11. [Student newspaper published at McNeese State University] (Winner of the cup at the College Writers Society of Louisiana, 6th Annual Meeting, 1958).

1960–1969

S-2 "Ronnie Comeaux: An Early Fragment." *Arena* 1 No. 2 (1961): 6-9. [Published by Sigma Tau Delta Honorary English Fraternity, McNeese State University].

S-3 "The Intruder." *The Sewanee Review* 7 No.2 (April-June 1963): 268-82. Collected in B-14.

S-4 "The Cross Country Runner." *Midwestern University Quarterly* 1 No. 4 (1966): 25-42.

S-5 "Love is the Sky." *Midwestern University Quarterly* 2 No.2 (1966): 18-36.

S-6 "The Blackberry Patch." In John William Corrington and Miller Williams, eds. *Southern Writing in the Sixties: Fiction.* Baton Rouge: Louisiana State University Press, 1966, pp. 108-15. Reprinted in Benjamin Forkner & Patrick Samway, eds. *Stories of the Modern South.* New York: Bantam, 1978, pp. 78-83.

S-7 "Over the Hill." *Sage* 11 No. 4 (Fall 1967): 255-66. Collected in B-2. Reprinted in Benjamin Forkner & Patrick Samway, eds. *Stories of the Modern South.* New York: Penguin, 1981, pp. 77-89.

S-8 "Madeline Sheppard." *Midwestern University Quarterly* 2 No. 4 (1967): 1-12.

S-9 "Andromache." *The New Yorker* 43 (January 6, 1968): 22-31. Collected in B-3.

S-10 "The Doctor." *The New Yorker* 45 (April 26, 1969): 38-9. Collected in B-2.

S-11 "If They Knew Yvonne." *North American Review* 254 No. 3 (Fall 1969): 18-28. Collected in B-2, B-11. Reprinted in Martha Foley & David Burnett, eds. *The Best American Short Stories.* Boston: Houghton Mifflin, 1970, pp. 84-107.

1970-1979

S-12 "Separate Flights." *North American Review* 255 No. 1 (Spring 1970): 10-26. Collected in B-2.

S-13 "Bless Me, Father." *The Carleton Miscellany* 11 No. 3 (Summer 1970): 78-88. Collected in B-5.

S-14 "In My Life." *Northwest Review* 11 No. 2 (1971): 20-25. Collected in B-2.

S-15 "The Dark Men." *Northwest Review* 12 No. 3 (1972): 3-13. Collected in B-4. Reprinted in Tom Jenks, ed. *Soldiers and Civilians.* New York: Scribner's, 1987, pp. 80-89.

S-16 "An Afternoon With the Old Man." *The New Yorker* 48 (September 2, 1972): 27-30. Collected in B-3.

S-17 "Corporal of Artillery." *Ploughshares* 1 No. 4 (1973): 8-13. Collected in B-3.

S-18 "The Shooting." *The Carleton Miscellany* 14 No. 1 (Fall-Winter 1973-74): 49-60. Collected in B-3.

S-19 "Goodbye." *Ploughshares* 2 No. 2 (1974): 61-69. Collected in B-5.

S-20 "Going Under." *North American Review* 259 (Spring 1974): 52-62. Collected in B-2, B-11.

S-21 "Cadence." *The Sewanee Review* 82 No. 3 (Summer 1974): 433-56.Collected in B-3. Reprinted in Martha Foley, ed. *The Best American Short Stories 1976*. Boston: Houghton Mifflin, 1975, pp. 80-99.

S-22 "The Bully." *The Sewanee Review* 83 No. 3 (Summer 1975): 394-405. Collected in B-3. Reprinted in Thomas Bonner, Jr. and Robert E. Skinner, eds. *Above Ground: Stories About Life and Death by New Southern Writers*. New Orleans, Xavier Review Press, 1993, pp. 35-44.

S-23 "We Don't Live Here Anymore." First appearance in *Separate Flights*. Boston: Godine, 1975, pp. 1-75. Collected in B-2, B-6.

S-24 "The Misogamist." *Penthouse* 8 No. 1 (September 1976): 70-72, 74, 114, 146. Note: This version not acknowledged by Dubus, it having been heavily edited without his knowledge or consent. His original version published for the first time in B-4.

S-25 "Contrition." *The North American Review* 261 (Winter 1976): 21-26. Collected in B-3.

S-26 "Adultery." *The Sewanee Review* 85 No. 1 (Winter 1977): 46-103. Collected in B-3, B-6, B-11.

S-27 "Delivering." *Harper's* 257 No. 1541 (October 1978): 78-80, 181-83. Collected in B-4, B-11.

S-28 "His Lover." *The William & Mary Review* 17 No. 1 (Fall 1978): 8-11. Collected in B-4.

S-29 "The Fat Girl." In Bill Henderson, ed. *The Pushcart Prize III: Best of the Small Presses.* Wainscott, NY: Pushcart Press, 1978-79, pp. 357-71. Collected in B-3, B-11. Reprinted in Raymond Carver and Tom Jenks, eds. *Short Story Masterpieces.* New York: Bantam, 1987. Note: Some evidence exists that an unacknowledged version of this story first appeared in *Playgirl.* Not seen.

S-30 "The Pitcher." *The North American Review* 264 No. 1 (Spring 1979): 18-24. Collected in B-4, B-11. Reprinted in William Abrahams, ed. *Prize Stories 1980: The O. Henry Awards.* New York: Doubleday, 1980, pp. 373-88.

S-31 "Waiting." *The Paris Review* 21 (Spring 1979): 114-20. Collected in B-4, B-11.

S-32 "Killings." *The Sewanee Review* 87 No. 2 (Spring 1979): 197-218. Collected in B-4, B-11.

S-33 "At St. Croix." *Ploughshares* 5 No. 3 (1979): 59-62. Collected in B-4. Reprinted in Dewitt Henry, ed. *The Ploughshares Reader: New Fiction for the Eighties.* Wainscott, NY: Pushcart Press, 1985, pp. 232-242.

1980-1989

S-34 "The Winter Father." *The Sewanee Review* 88 No. 2 (Spring 1980): 155-75. Collected in B-4, B-11. Reprinted in Hortense Calisher with Shannon Ravenel, eds. *The Best American Short Stories, 1981.* Boston: Houghton Mifflin, 1981, pp. 129-49.

S-35 "Finding A Girl in America." First appearance in *Finding A Girl in America.* Boston: Godine, 1980, pp. 129-83. Collected in B-4, B-6.

S-36 "Anna." *Playboy* 28 No. 6 (June 1981): 137, 174, 236, 238, 240, 242, 246, 248, 251, 253. Collected in B-5, B-11.

S-37 "The New Boy." *Harper's* 264 (January 1982): 50-56, 58-60. Collected in B-5.

S-38 "The Captain." *Ploughshares* 8 No. 4 (1982): 219-35. Collected in B-5, B-11.

S-39 "A Father's Story." *The Black Warrior Review* 9 No. 2 (Spring 1983): 7-24. Collected in B-5, B-11. Reprinted in John Updike with Shannon Ravenel, eds. *The Best American Short Stories, 1984*. Boston, Houghton Mifflin, 1984.

S-40 "After the Game." *Fiction Network* 1 (Fall 1983): 15-19. Not seen.Collected in B-9, B-11. Reprinted in Scott Walker, ed. *The Graywolf Annual: Short Stories*. Port Townsend, WA: Graywolf Press, 1985, pp. 15-23.

S-41 "Sorrowful Mysteries." *Crazy Horse* No. 25 (Fall 1983): 83-94. Collected in B-5, B-11.

S-42 "The Pretty Girl." First appearance in Dubus, *The Times Are Never So Bad*. Boston: Godine, 1983, pp. 3-59. Collected in B-5, B-6, B-11.

S-43 "Land Where My Fathers Died." *Antaeus* 53 (Autumn 1984): 190-233. Collected in B-9. Printed separately as a signed limited edition. See B-7.Reprinted in George Murphy, ed. *The Best Short Fiction for 1985: The Editor's Choice: New American Stories*. New York: Bantam, 1986, pp. 66-104.

S-44 "Rose." *Ploughshares* 11 No. 2-3 (1985): 11-51. Collected in B-9, B-11. Reprinted in Bill Henderson, ed. *The Pushcart Prize, XI: Best of the Small Presses*. Wainscott, NY: Pushcart Press, 1986-87, pp. 116-49.

S-45 "Molly." *Crazyhorse* No. 30 (Spring 1986): 86-139. Collected in B-9.

S-46 "Deaths at Sea." *Quarterly West* No. 22 (Spring/Summer 1986): 71-116. Collected in B-9.

S-47 "Dressed Like Summer Leaves." *The Sewanee Review* 94 No. 4 (Fall 1986): 541-54. Collected in B-9.

S-48 "Blessings." *Yankee* 50 No. 10 (October 1986): 88-93, 156, 158, 160, 162, 164, 166, 168, 170-71. Printed separately as a signed limited edition. See B-10. Collected in B-14.

S-49 "They Now Live in Texas." *Indiana Review* 10 No. 1-2 (1987): 3-6. Collected in B-11.

S-50 "The Curse." *Playboy* 35 No. 1 (January 1988): 126-27, 179-80. Not seen. Collected in B-11.

S-51 "Her Smile." *Gentleman's Quarterly* 58 (November 1988): 251-2. Not seen.

S-52 "Miranda Over the Valley." In *Selected Stories*. Boston, Godine, 1988. Collected in B-2, B-11. Note: Some evidence exists that an unacknowledged version of this story first appeared in *Viva*. Not seen.

1990-1999

S-53 "Sunday Morning." *Boston Review* 15 No. 6 (December 1990): 24-25. Collected in B-14.

S-54 "The Lover." *Ploughshares* 17 No. 2-3 (Fall 1991): 189-97. Collected in B-14.

S-55 "In the Quiet." *Yankee* 56 (August 1992): 50-3+ Not seen.

S-56 "Woman On A Plane." *Ploughshares* 18 No. 2-3 (Fall 1992): 64-67. Collected in B-14.

S-57 "The Colonel's Wife." *Playboy* 40 No. 1 (January 1993): 110-12, 190-93. Collected in B-14. Reprinted in *Ten Tales*. Huntington Beach, CA: James Cahill Publishing, 1994 [limited to a printing of 250 copies]. Not seen.

S-58 "The Last Moon." *Yankee* 59 (January 1995): 62-7. Collected in B-14.

S-59 "All the Time in the World." *Epoch* 44 No. 1 (1995): 8-17. Collected in B-14.

S-60 "Falling in Love." *War, Literature & the Arts* 7 No. 2 (Fall/Winter 1995): 83-94. Collected in B-14.

S-61 "Out of the Snow." *Yankee* 59 (December 1995): 50-3+, continued in *Yankee* 60 (January 1996): 78-81+ Not seen. Collected in B-14.

S-62 "Dancing After Hours." *Epoch* 45 No. 1 (1996): 8-35. Collected in B-14.

S-63 "The Timing of Sin." *Esquire* 125 (March 1996): 120-6, 128. Collected in B-14.

S-64 "At Night." *Yankee* 61 (February 1997): 94-5. Collected in B-14.

S-65 "Riding North." *Oxford Magazine* 12 (Spring-Summer 1998): 92-120.

S-66 "Corporal Lewis." *Epoch* 48 No. 3 (1999): 168-69.

Unverified

The following stories are cited in Dubus collections as having previously appeared in magazines.

S-67 "Graduation." Collected in B-3, B-11. Cited as having been previously published in *New Dawn Magazine*. Several magazines have existed with this title, but investigation failed to even determine which actually published the story.

S-68 "Townies." Collected in B-4, B-11. Cited as having been previously published in *The Real Paper*. The title has been identified as an underground tabloid newspaper formerly published in Massachusetts. It is no longer in print, and most libraries reporting holdings own it in the form of a special underground newspaper microfilm collection.

S-69 "A Love Song." Collected in B-14. Cited as having previously appeared in *Crazyhorse*. Searches of copies held in local collections proved fruitless, as did interlibrary loan. Help was not forthcoming through the magazine's editorial office.

S-70 "Leslie in California." Collected in B-5, B-11, B-13. Later republished as a separate signed limited edition (see B-9). Cited as having originally appeared in *Redbook*. Searches of copies held in local collections proved fruitless. Help was not forthcoming from the magazine's editorial office.

Section 2

Fiction-Books

B-1 *The Lieutenant.* New York: The Dial Press, 1967. Verso of title page reads, *First Printing, 1967.* First paperback printing by Dell, Number 4779. Verso of title page reads, "First Dell Printing—November 1968."

B-2 *Separate Flights: A Novella and Seven Short Stories.* Boston: David R. Godine, 1975. Verso of title page reads, "First published in 1975 by David R. Godine, Publisher." Includes stories S-7, S-10, S-11, S-12, S-14, S-20, S-23, S-52.

B-3 *Adultery and Other Choices: Nine Short Stories and a Novella.* Boston: David R. Godine, 1977.Verso of title page reads, "*First Published in 1977 by David R. Godine, Publisher.*" Includes stories S-9, S-16, S-17, S-18, S-21, S-22, S-25, S-26, S-29, S-67.

B-4 *Finding a Girl in America: Ten Stories & A Novella.* Boston: David R. Godine, Publisher, 1980.Verso of title pages reads, "*First published in 1980 by David R. Godine, Publisher, Inc.*" Includes stories S-15, S-24, S-27, S-28, S-30, S-31, S-32, S-33, S-34, S-35, S-68.

B-5 *The Times Are Never So Bad: A Novella & Eight Short Stories.* Boston: David R. Godine, 1983. Verso of title page reads, "*First published in 1983 by David R. Godine, Publisher, Inc.*" and "First edition." Includes stories S-13, S-19, S-36, S-37, S-38, S-39, S-41, S-42, S-70.

B-6 *We Don't Live Here Anymore: The Novellas of Andre Dubus.* New York: Crown Publishers, 1984.Verso of title page reads, 10 9 8 7 6 5 4 3 2 1 and "First Edition." Includes stories S-23, S-26, S-35, S-42.

B-7 *Land Where My Fathers Died.* (N.P.) Stuart Wright, Publisher, 1984. Verso of title pages reads, "First Edition." Unnumbered page 39 reads, "THIS EDITION IS LIMITED TO 200 COPIES" Reprints S-44 in its entirety.

B-8 *Voices From The Moon.* Boston: David R. Godine, Publisher, 1984. Verso of title page reads, *"First edition published in 1984 by David R. Godine, Publisher, Inc."* and "First edition." Collected in B-11.

B-9 *The Last Worthless Evening: Four Novellas & Two Stories.* Boston: David R. Godine, Publisher, 1986. Verso of title page reads, "First edition published in 1986 by *David R. Godine, Publisher, Inc."* and "FIRST EDITION." Includes stories S-40, S-43, S-44, S-45, S-46, S-47.

B-10 *Blessings.* Elmwood, CT: Raven Editions, 1987. Verso of title page reads, "An Abridged edition of this work first appeared in Yankee." Separate notation reads, "Limited to 70 copies. Numbered copies 1-60 are hand bound in paper over boards, and 10 presentation copies *hors commerce* are hand bound in quarter leather with paper over boards. All copies are signed by the author." Not seen. First separate appearance of S-48.

B-11 *Selected Stories.* Boston: David R. Godine, Publisher, 1988. Verso of title pages reads, "First published in 1988 by David R. Godine, Publisher, Inc." and "First Edition." Includes stories S-11, S-21, S-26, S-27, S-29, S-30, S-31, S-32, S-34, S-36, S-38, S-39, S-40, S-41, S-42, S-45, S-49, S-50, S-52, S-67, S-68, S-70 and B-6.

B-12 *Into the Silence: American Stories.* Cambridge, MA: The Green Street Press, 1988. (Edited by Dubus, his only direct contribution is a brief introductory essay. See E-22.).

B-13 *Leslie in California.* Otisville, NY: Birch Brook Press, 1989. Facing title page reads, "A brief book designed, typeset & printed at Birch Brook Press, Otisville, NY Copyright 1989." Verso of title page reads, "First edition." First separate appearance. Reprints S-70 in its entirety.

B-14 *Dancing After Hours.* New York: Alfred A. Knopf, 1996. Verso of title pages reads, "FIRST EDITION." Includes stories S-3, S-48, S-53, S-54, S-56, S-57, S-58, S-59, S-60, S-61, S-62, S-63, S-64, S-69.

Section 3

Essays—first periodical appearances

1950-1959

E-1"The Way I Feel." *The Contraband* (McNeese State University).
This column appeared in the following issues.

16 No. 3 (September 28, 1954): 2.
16 No. 5 (October 12, 1954): 2.
16 No. 6 (October 19, 1954): 4.
16 No. 7 (October 26, 1954): 2.
16 No. 8 (November 2, 1954): 7.
16 No. 9 (November 9, 1954): 4.
16 No. 10 (November 16, 1954): 2.
16 No. 13 (December 7, 1954): 6.
16 No. 14 (December 14, 1954): 2.
16 No. 15 (January 11, 1955): 2.
16 No. 17 (February 1, 1955): 2, 6.
16 No. 18 (February 8, 1955): 2-3.
16 No. 19 (February 15, 1955): 6.
16 No. 20 (February 22, 1955): 4.
16 No. 21 (March 1, 1955): 4.
16 No. 22 (March 8, 1955): 4.
16 No. 23 (March 22, 1955): 11.
16 No. 24 (March 29, 1955): 3.
16 No. 25 (April 5, 1955): 6.
16 No. 26 (April 19, 1955): 4.
16 No. 27 (April 26, 1955): 6.
16 No. 29 (May 10, 1955): 4.
17 No. 1 (September 20, 1955): 4.
17 No. 2 (September 27, 1955): 4.
17 No. 3 (October 4, 1955): 4.
17 No. 4 (October 11, 1955): 2.
17 No. 6 (October 25, 1955): 6.
17 No. 7 (November 1, 1955): 2.
17 No. 8 (November 8, 1955): 2.

17 No. 13 (January 10, 1956): 2.
17 No. 15 (February 7, 1956): 6.
17 No. 24 (April 17, 1956): 4.
17 No. 29 (May 25, 1956): 8.

E-2 "Pop Skips Vacation Because He Likes It Here." *The Contraband* 16 No. 14 (December 14, 1954): 11.

E-3 "Bayou Players Score Hit in Wilde." *The Contraband* 16 No. 27 (April 26, 1955): 27.

E-4 "Andre Dubus Sets Keynote for S-O Week at MSC." *The Contraband* 17 No. 11 (December 6, 1955): 1-2.

1970-1979

E-5 "Paths to Redemption: Walker Percy's *Lancelot.*" *Harper's* 254 No. 1523 (April 1977): 86-88.

E-6 "Footnotes: Running for Your Life." *Boston Magazine* 69 No. 10 (October 1977): 203-4. Collected in N-1.

E-7 "Reading: Fiction and the Facts of Life." *Boston Magazine* 69 No. 11 (November 1977): 58, 60, 62.

E-8 "Of Robin Hood and Womanhood." *Boston Magazine* 69 No. 12 (December 1977): 233-36. Collected in N-1.

E-9 "At Random: Packing It In." *Boston Magazine* 70 No. 1 (January 1978): 163-64.

E-10 "The Sounds of Silence." *Boston Magazine* 70 No. 2 (February 1978): 64, 90-91.

E-11 "Footnotes: To Make a Long Story Short." *Boston Magazine* 70 No. 2 (February 1978): 122-24.

E-12 "Manners: The End of a Season." *Boston Magazine* 70 No. 10 (October 1978): 94-95. Collected in N-1.

E-13 "Railroad Sketches." *Boston Magazine* 75 No. 1 (January 1983): 214, 174-178. Collected in N-1.

E-14 "A Laurel for Richard Hugo." *Black Warrior Review* 9 No. 2 (Spring 1983): 104-5.

E-15 "Literature." *America* 151 No.5 (September 1-8, 1984): 106, 108-9.

E-16 "Two Ghosts." *Mid-American Review* 5 No. 2 (1985): 27-32. Collected in N-1.

E-17 "After Twenty Years." *North American Review* 271 No. 4 (December 1986): 60-61. Collected in N-1.

E-18 "Intensive Care." *Indiana Review* 10 No. 1-2 (Spring 1987): 7-8. Collected in N-1.

E-19 "Lights of the Long Night." *Black Warrior Review* 14 No. 1 (Fall 1987): 13-15. Collected in N-1.

E-20 "The Judge and Other Snakes." *Boston Magazine* 80 No. 5 (May 1988): 139, 172-79. Collected in N-1.

E-21 "Broken Vessels." *New York Times Magazine* (November 20, 1988): 116. Collected in N-1. Cited in *Broken Vessels* (1991) as having previously appeared in a "condensed form" in a periodical named *Special Report*. This version not seen.

E-22 "Into the Silence." In Andre Dubus, ed. *Into the Silence*. Green Street Press, 1988, pp. 3-5. (Note: the brief essay is an introduction to a collection of stories edited by Dubus. See B-12).

E-23 "A Salute to Mister Yates." *Black Warrior Review* 15 No. 2 (Spring 1989): 160-61. Collected in N-1. Also collected in N-2, retitled "Good-bye to Richard Yates."

E-24 "Bastille Day." *Yankee* 53 No. 7 (July 1989): 68+. Not seen. Collected in N-1.

1990-1999

E-25 "Breathing." *Epoch* 40 No. 1 (1991): 20. Collected in N-1.

E-26 "Sketches at Home." *Epoch* 40 No. 1 (1991): 21-26. Collected in N-1.

E-27 "Husbands." *Epoch* 40 No. 1 (1991): 27-33. Collected in N-1. Reprinted in *Harper's* 283 No. 1696 (September 1991): 35, 38, 40-1.

E-28 "Legs." *The Southern Review* 28 No. 4 (October 1992): 737. Collected in N-2.

E-29 "Grace." *The Southern Review* 28 No. 4 (October 1992): 737-8. Collected in N-2.

E-30 "Autumn Legs." *The Southern Review* 28 No. 4 (October 1992): 738-40. Collected in N-2.

E-31 "Carrying." *The Boston Globe Sunday Magazine* (January 10, 1993): 14. Collected in N-2.

E-32 "Out of the Darkness. *Health* 7 (March/April 1993): 106, 108. Collected in N-2, retitled "About Kathryn."

E-33 "A Quiet Seige: The Death and Life of a Gay Naval Officer." *Harper's* 286 No. 1717 (June 1993): 56-61. Collected in N-2, retitled "Imperiled Men."

E-34 "The Eternal Supper." *Portland Magazine* 12 No. 3 (Autumn 1993): 16-19. Collected in N-2, retitled "Communion."

E-35 Untitled tribute. In *Richard Yates, An American Writer: Tributes in Memorium.* New York: Seymour Lawrence, 1993, p. 27.

E-36 "Liv Ullman in Spring." *Yankee 58* (April 1994): 92-7+. Not seen. Collected in N-2.

E-37 "Progress Notes." *U. S. Catholic* 59 No. 8 (August 1994): 30. Collected in N-1.

E-38 "At the Algonquin." *The Sewanee Review* 103 No. 1 (Winter 1995): 123-27. Collected in N-2, retitled "Mailer at the Algonquin."

E-39 "A Faith Journey." *Portland Magazine* 14 No. 1 (Spring 1995): 22-25. Collected in N-2, retitled "Sacraments."

E-40 "Love in the Morning." *DoubleTake* No. 3 (Winter 1996): 7. Collected in N-2.

E-41 "At the Altar: Girl." *Portland Magazine* 15 No. 1 (Spring 1996): 18. Collected in N-2, retitled "Girls."

E-42 "Song of Pity." *Epoch* 46 No. 1 (1997): 89-94. A different version of this essay appears as "Crip Sheet" in *Utne Reader* No. 83 (September/ October 1997): 35-6. Collected in N-2.

E-43 "At Night." *Yankee* 61 (February 1997): 94-5. Not seen.

E-44 "Giving Up the Gun." *The New Yorker* 73 No. 2 (February 24- March 3, 1997): 84-90. Collected in N-2. Reprinted in Judith A. Standford, ed. *Responding to Literature*. Mountain View, CA: Mayfield Publishing Company, Third Edition, 1999. pp. 483-90.

E-45 "A Hemingway Story." *The Kenyon Review* 19 No. 2 (Spring 1997): 141-8. Collected in N-2.

E-46 "Witness." *The New Yorker* 73 No. 20 (July 21, 1997): 33-6. Collected in N-2.

E-47 "Digging." *Epoch* 46 No. 3 (1997): 407-14. Collected in N-2.

E-48 "Messages." *The Boston Globe Sunday Magazine* (September 14, 1997): 10. (Note: This essay is part of a group of essays published under the title of "Lost and Found: Variations on a Theme by Five New England Writers." The writers include Alice Hoffman, Sue Miller, Dubus, Gish Jen, and Geoffrey Wolff.) Collected in N-2.

E-49 "Brothers." *Salon* October 8, 1997). <www.salon.com/music/ feature/1997/10/cov_8dubus. html> and <www.salon.com/music/ feature/1997/10/cov_08dubus.2html> Collected in N-2.

E-50 "First Books." In Ken Lopez [compiler] *Authors' Firsts: A Catalog of First Books, First Fiction, First Novels.* Hadley, MA: Ken Lopez, Bookseller, 1997, pp. [1-2]. Verso of front cover reads, "Copyright 1997 Ken Lopez/Introduction Copyright 1997 Andre Dubus." Collected in N-2.

E-51 "Letter to a Young Writer." *Epoch* 47 No. 2-3 (1998): 262-66. Collected in N-2.

E-52 "A Man Named Father Clarence Stanghon." *Literary Review* 42 No. 1 (Fall 1998): 43-4.

E-53 "Letter to a Writers' Workshop." In *Meditations from a Movable Chair: Essays.* New York, Knopf, 1998. First appearance in N-2.

E-54 "Letter to Amtrak." In *Meditations from a Movable Chair: Essays.* New York: Knopf, 1998. First appearance in N-2.

2000-

E-55 "A Country Road Song." *Yankee* 64 (February 2000): 66-71.

Unverified

The following essays are cited in Dubus collections as having previously appeared in magazines.

E-56 "Out Like a Lamb" Collected in N-1. Cited as having previously appeared in *Boston Magazine.* A search of the magazine in the collection of Boston College proved fruitless. The magazine's editorial office reported that they had no internal index or backfiles through which they could determine prior publication.

E-57 "On Charon's Wharf." Collected in N-1. Cited as having previously appeared in *Boston Magazine.*

E-58 "Selling Stories." Collected in N-1. Cited as having previously appeared in *Boston Magazine.*

E-59 "Marketing." Collected in N-1. Cited as having previously appeared in *Boston Magazine.*

E-60 "Under the Lights." Collected in N-1. Cited as having previously appeared in *Village Voice*. The *Voice* is not indexed, and the editorial office reported no internal index to their back issues.

E-61 "A Woman in April." Collected in N-1. Cited as having previously appeared in *Gentleman's Quarterly*. Citation not identified, and help from the editorial office was not forthcoming.

E-62. "Bodily Mysteries." Collected in N-2. Cited as having previously appeared in a publication entitled *Special Report*. This is such a common title that it has not yet been possible to positively identify the magazine or locate an editorial office.

Section 4

Nonfiction Books

N-1 *Broken Vessels*. Introduction by Tobias Wolff. Boston: David R. Godine, Publisher. 1991. Verso of title page reads, FIRST EDITION. Includes essays E-5, E-8, E-12, E-13, E-16, E-17, E-18, E-19, E-20, E-21, E-23, E-24, E-25, E-26, E-27, E-37, E-56, E-57, E-58, E-59. E-60, E-61.

N-2 *Meditations from a Movable Chair: Essays*. New York: Alfred A. Knopf, 1998. Verso of title page reads, "First Edition." Includes essays E-23, E-28, E-29, E-30, E-31, E-32, E-33, E-34, E-38, E-39, E-40, E-41, E-42, E-44, E-45, E-46, E-47, E-48, E-49, E-50, E-51, E-53, E-54, E-62.

Acknowledgements

Even in these times, when much of the world's knowledge is almost instantaneously available through the World Wide Web, assembling a comprehensive, accurate bibliography of a creative writer requires a patience and powers of deductive reasoning that might tax the capacity of a Sherlock Holmes.

When library collections in my geographic region failed to own titles or issues I required, and I lacked sufficient information to rely on interlibrary loan, I turned in many cases to university archivists and librarians, and to the editors of magazines in which Dubus' work had appeared. While not everyone proved cooperative, most did, and the bibliography would not be complete without recognition of their invaluable help.

Chief among this group of people are the stewards of the only extant archival collections devoted to Dubus, University Archivist Lester G. Sullivan and Associate Archivist Irwin Lachoff at Xavier University of Louisiana, and Kathie Bordelon, University Archivist at McNeese State University. Thanks to their searches of various databases and page-by-page investigations of titles without indexes, some virtually unknown early fiction and nonfiction has been rediscovered. McNeese State University Special Collections, in particular, has a substantial record of Dubus' fiction and nonfiction published while he was an undergraduate student.

In a similar regard, Xavier University Archives and Special Collections holds a number of unpublished stories and essays in manuscript. Since Dubus' death, some new fiction and nonfiction has appeared in print, but so far as is known, these pieces at Xavier are not in press anywhere at this time.

Other co-conspirators include

Bill Boles, Librarian, *The Boston Globe*, Boston, Massachusetts.

Jefferson Decker, Managing Editor, *Boston Review* (Massachusetts Institute of Technology), Cambridge, Massachusetts.

Daisy Dodge, Editor, *The Black Warrior Review* (University of Alabama), Tuscaloosa, Alabama.

Brian Doyle, *Portland Magazine* (University of Portland), Portland, Oregon.

Stacy Gould, Interim University Archivist, William and Mary College, Williamsburg, Virginia.

Melba S. Harvill, University Archivist, Midwestern State University, Wichita Falls, Texas.

Deborah Kennedy, *Oxford Magazine* (Miami University of Ohio), Oxford, Ohio.

R. Jay Magill, Jr., Associate Editor, *Double Take Magazine,* Somerville, Massachusetts.

Gregg Rosenblum, Assistant Editor, *Ploughshares* (Emerson College), Boston, Massachusetts.

Dr. Kwasi Sarkodie-Mensah, Boston College Libraries.

Jodie Saville, *Yankee Magazine.*

Margot Schilpp, Editor, *Quarterly West* (University of Utah), Salt Lake City, Utah.

Works Cited

[1] Andre Dubus, "Reading: Fiction and the Facts of Life," *Boston Magazine* 69 No. 11 (November 1977): 58.

[2] "Reading," 60.

[3] "Reading," 60.

[4] "Reading," 62.

[5] Andre Dubus, "Footnotes: To Make a Long Story Short." *Boston Magazine* 70 No. 2 (February 1978): 122.

[6] "Footnotes," 124.

Robert E. Skinner's works include *Two Guns from Harlem: The Detective Fiction of Chester Himes, Chester Himes: An Annotated Primary and Secondary Bibliography,* and essays on Elmore Leonard, Douglas C. Jones, and A.B. Guthrie, Jr., as well as five novels, the most recent of which is *Pale Shadow.* He is University Librarian at Xavier University of Louisiana, New Orleans.

Homily

the curtains;

he asked her to open them; he said he
was sorry, but the covered windows reminded
him of the hospital. The hospital had been
very difficult. He had served in two wars
without being injured, and had never
been confined to a hospital. Now when
he saw the curtains behind Lydia, he felt
enclosed by something that would ~~that~~
take away his breath.

100

He could wheel slowly down the
carpeted hall that began where the living
and dining rooms joined, but the hall was
too narrow for him to turn ~~into~~ into the
rooms it led to; one of them was a
bathroom. He longed for a shower, and
never felt truly clean. He kept a plastic
urinal hooked by its handle over a railing

"The Colonel's Wife"
2nd draft
Andre Dubus

Patrick Samway, S.J.

Meditative Thoughts on the Life of Andre Dubus

First there is the morning, a time of light and awakening. Light, a favorite image of St. John the Evangelist, brings newness and the energy to begin, to set out on the road. Then there is noon, a time to pause and gather strength. The pause restores our energies and we set out again to work on our projects and master the tasks at hand. Then there is evening, a time to retire and pull together our lives, to offer thanksgiving, and plan for the next day. The third chapter of the Book of Quoleth in the Jewish Bible simply and matter-of-factly reminds us:

> For everything there is a season,
> and a time for every matter under heaven:
> a time to be born, and a time to die;
> a time to plant, and a time to pluck up what is planted . . .
> a time to break down, and a time to build up;
> a time to weep and a time to laugh;
> a time to mourn, and a time to dance. . . .

These words from Scripture recall that there is a rhythm to the world of nature and to our lives. Nor do we find it difficult to accept this rhythm. There is morning. There is noon. There is evening.

We gather today to celebrate the life of a special person, our brother Andre Dubus, and to remind ourselves, since we are people who tend to forget so easily, that in and through the resurrection of Jesus the Christ, death has no sting, no control over us, and we are not to fear the dark. Rather we are children of the light. Thus today is a day of victory. This does not mean that at every moment of our waking hours we feel good or perceive life as a constant blessing; we are too wise for that and we have come too far to be pollyannaish in our thoughts and attitudes. No matter how much we suffer or how many shadowy days we experience, the Lord guides us and gives us the light and warmth we need to see and grow. Be not of little faith.

Kathyrn, Beth, Patricia, Peggy, Suzanne, Tom, Andre, Fontaine, Jeb, Victoria, Nicole, Susan, Cadence, Madeleine, Ethan, Theo, Austin, Ariadne, and Elias grew and were nourished by Andre's love. Jack will miss Andre, his "bro," as he called him, and Phil will miss the presence of a dear, dear friend. Andre touched their lives, and the lives of all of us, in ways that each one of us will continually cherish. In his essay entitled "Broken Vessels" in the book *Broken Vessels*, Andre writes of explaining to Cadence some of the difficult moments in his life—and in her life too. He told her that someday she would be a strong, brave woman. "Tears flowed down her cheeks," he wrote, "but she was quiet and her eyes were shining, and her face was like a woman's receiving love and praise." We all grieve; yet we take courage in knowing that Andre is beyond pain and loss.

In the Bible, Isaiah speaks not only to those Jews who were held hostage in Babylon, but to us today. It is the Lord who gives us release, who calls us to himself. "Go up on a high mountain / joyful messenger to Zion. / Shout with a loud voice, / messenger to Jerusalem. / Shout without fear, say to the towns of Judah, / 'Here is your God.'" Just as the Lord gathers his sheep into his arms and takes them to the sheepfold, so too he will gather those who have died and lead them from captivity to the New Jerusalem. Isaiah had reason to celebrate: The Lord has brought about a new creation and formed a new people who are his own. As Psalm 8 notes, the Lord's new creatures, his chosen ones, are crowned with glory and splendor. And so I say, ever so gently, be not of little faith.

By some standards, the life of Andre Dubus was long and not long, a brief 62 years when we consider how old we are as a human race. I knew him as a lovely and loving human being, who often reminded me of the words of a fellow Jesuit, Gerard Manley Hopkins:

> . . . the just man justices;
> Kéeps grace: thát keeps all his goings graces;
> Acts in God's eye what in God's eye he is—
> Christ—for Christ plays in ten thousand places,
> Lovely in limbs, and lovely in eyes not his,
> To the Father through the features of men's faces.

Andre worked hard as a master craftsman of the written word, as witnessed by his two novels, eight volumes of novellas and stories, and essays in *Broken Vessels* and *Meditations From a Movable Chair*. He once told me that he often read his stories aloud into a tape recorder and then listened back to them; when the words had the sound of a fork striking expensive crystal, he knew the stories were finished. Andre's heart heard what his ghost guessed. I saw Andre in enough varying circumstances—from long discussions during several agonizing days in Mass General in 1986 to an analysis of Mo Vaughn's batting record at Fenway Park last summer—to know that wherever he was, whether touching bottom or reaching the top or somewhere in between, his life was centered on Jesus the Christ. I remember one time years ago when he and Peggy and Cadence were living in Tuscaloosa, where Andre was a writer-in-residence at the state university. Andre and I were sitting in old-fashioned rocking chairs on the side porch of their house enjoying the waning Alabama sun, talking and swapping stories. Andre told me that he knew what he wanted to do, but he had no map to get him there. He felt he could not teach any more, since he had so poured himself into his work at Bradford that his doctor said it was not prudent for him to return to the classroom. And so, we put down our J.D.'s, and silently prayed for a few minutes. I told him I would continue to remember him in my prayers, as I did. About two weeks later, Andre called and said that he had been granted a Guggenheim, just one of the wonderful recognitions that came his way, and wanted to know what prayers I had said, because he had a few more high-ticket requests to make.

Andre knew that this life is too much trouble, far too strange, to arrive at the end of it and then be asked what you make of it and have to answer, "Scientific humanism." That wouldn't do. A poor show. Rather, as Walker Percy once wrote, life is a mystery, love is a delight. Therefore, Andre took it as axiomatic that one should settle for nothing less than infinite mystery and the infinite delight; i.e., God. In fact, he demanded it. He refused to settle for anything less. And at his death, the Lord of Hosts welcomed him and blessed him; he now lives in infinite mystery and infinite delight. There is a time to mourn and a time to weep. And there is a time to rededicate ourselves to our own tasks at hand, knowing that we have understood a bit more, in and through the life, death, and resurrection of Andre Dubus, God's mysterious plans for each one of us. Let every valley be filled in, let every cliff become a plain, let every ridge become a valley. We now walk more confidently with the Lord of all to our final home.

—Haverhill, Massachusetts, March 1, 1999

Afterword

of the bed, and Lydia emptied and cleaned it. For most of his four weeks and five days in the hospital, he had to use a bedpan, and nurses cleaned him. In his last week, the physical therapist and a nurse helped him from his wheelchair on to a hospital commode; they removed the inside arms from the chair and the commode, pushed the transfer board under him, and held his legs as he moved across. Then they propped his legs on pillows on a chair and left him alone. He had to use both hands to push himself up from the seat, so when the two women returned they had to hold his legs and lifted him,

"The Colonel's Wife"
2nd draft

Andre Dubus

Tobias Wolff

Sissies Anonymous

The first time I ever laid eyes on Andre Dubus he was bearing down on me at a party. He didn't trouble to stop and introduce himself, no, he bent over my chair and in front of everyone kissed me on the mouth. I recoiled like a howitzer. "Hah!" he said. "Homosexual terror!" and laughed hugely. I was so shocked that I started laughing too. And what made him want to do such a thing?—Ah, he'd liked a story of mine. There are other ways of showing appreciation, and I mostly prefer them to this way, but he somehow put me off balance and managed to keep me off balance for the next twenty years.

Andre called me Silent Death. When I picked up the phone and heard just those words, spoken in his gravelly drawl—"Silent Death"—I wanted to scream. I'd told him truly and repeatedly that my service in Vietnam had not been at all heroic or even competent, but it pleased Andre to affect disbelief, indeed to treat my very denials as proof that I had carried the war to the enemy with implacable and dire efficiency. So when I heard those words I wanted to scream but it always came out in laughter. There is generally an element of self-importance in self-deprecation, and Andre knew where to put the needle.

He could also apply the needle to himself. Andre had about him a loud blustering maleness—one of my sons, then quite young, called him Yosemite Sam—and enough binocular vision to see the sometimes cartoonish aspects of his own manner. I visited him in Haverhill one night after the accident and found him wheeling around the house in a Rambo headband and a Marine Corps t-shirt with his old Expert Rifleman's badge pinned over his heart. It was both self-parodic and serious; Andre was intensely and rightly proud of his years in the Marines, even while having a complex, illusionless sense of the limitations of military life and the unacknowledged motives that send men into it. The Marine Corps, he maintained, was basically a collection of sissies trying to prove they weren't. We sometimes talked of starting a Sissies Anonymous chapter, stocked with former jarheads and fighter pilots and paratroopers and SEALS who would, with tears and breaking voices, stand and testify to the pain of their double lives: My name is Moose Steel, and I'm a recovering sissy . . .

Andre had a very soft heart under that hairy chest, which didn't stop him from peeling off his shirt when the mood struck him. At a literary festival in Athens, Ohio, he was taking questions after reading one of his stories, and as was his habit he sailed off onto subjects of his own, and soon went aground on Women's Liberation. I saw it about to happen and my heart sank because though it was clear that Andre also saw the reefs looming he was happily resolved to drive upon them. He held forth for a good half hour while the men in the audience cringed at what we imagined to be the women's wrath at Andre's observation (to cite but one) that the entire result of Women's Lib was that women could now "wear suits and take the train to work and tell lies all day." And yet at the end it was the women who were laughing, and laughing hard; they could recognize a bravura riff when they heard one.

Yet there was some conviction in what he said. Andre hated a bully more than anything. And so he distrusted what turns people into bullies—power. In Andre's view, the power men had hogged for themselves was no prize at all; it soured their natures, made them vain and greedy and dishonest. Wearing suits and telling lies all day was pretty much how he saw the world of business and government that women were trying to break into. Paradoxically, it was his sense of women as having better or at least more interesting characters than men that led him to look skeptically on their struggle for power.

This was paternalism, of course, but of a different temper than most I've seen. It didn't proceed from any desire to protect his own position in the world. It came really from his love for women, a love they returned. There was always a company of them in attendance at the house—daughters, daughters-in-law, granddaughters, ex-wives, friends, fellow writers, former students, admiring readers paying their respects. Once a week for several years he led a workshop, gratis, for a group of girls from a local shelter. He helped women writers in every way he could. And he wrote better about women than any man of his generation, both from their point of view and from without. He wrote about mothers and daughters, women in love, women being beaten, women being raped, women being stalked, women working, women being friends with other women, women loving their husbands and committing adultery and saving themselves and their children from bad men. Each of his women is particular and unexpected, her moral and physical nature without a shadow of male fantasy or condescension.

And yet, and yet. The desire to protect what we love can do great harm to what we love, as we see in Andre's masterful "A Father's Story," in which the pious, likeable narrator, Luke Ripley, arranges a cover-up for his daughter after she accidentally kills a boy with her car while out drinking. Luke does a terrible thing here, not so much in concealing his daughter's culpability as in removing her from the process of confession and acceptance of punishment that is her only road back into the human community. Luke may have saved her from legal retribution, but he has isolated her forever with her unexpiated guilt. It is an unwittingly arrogant, profoundly destructive act, and though Luke feels true compassion for the dead boy and his parents, he has no sense of what he has done to his daughter. On the contrary, he likens his love for her to God's love for him, a breathtaking flourish of pride. The story is a shrewd portrait of a man confounding his desire to save his daughter by smothering her spirit in the name of love, never once imagining that a greater love would allow her the freedom to act responsibly and redeem herself.

There is a muddle of love and self-contradiction at the heart of this great story, as in Andre's heart. For all his swagger and volume, I never saw a man so tender with his friends or for that matter with anyone who seemed in need of it. He was very brave, yet prone to question his own bravery, its true motive and effect. I can't begin to describe even the little I saw of his courage after the accident, as he lost command of the sturdy body he'd taken such delight in, and had to begin life anew; so here is a story on a more comprehensible scale. We were leaving a bar in Bradford one snowy night and found the wheelchair exit blocked by a truck. We had the bartender ask—loudly, repeatedly—whose truck it was. No one answered. We finally gave up, and Andre's son, Andre III, and some other friends and I carried him up the steps and outside. While we were saying our good-byes in the parking lot the bartender himself came out, and, not seeing us, got some cigarettes out of the truck. It was his, the prick! He was a big guy but Andre wheeled at him in a fury, daring him to stand. The bartender ran around the lot a while and finally made it back inside. The rest of us were giddy with the pleasure of seeing him humiliated, but Andre was embarrassed at what he'd done. Later, perhaps with this night in mind, he wrote: "If you confront a man from a wheelchair you're bullying him."

He was both ribald and gallant; hilariously profane, and true to his Catholic faith—toward the end of his life he was receiving communion every day. He loved earthy jokes and conversation, but never at the expense of an actual person; Andre didn't tear down other people, either in argument or gossip. He'd always been a big man. In the wheelchair he grew even bigger.

Uproarious as he was, he was also courtly and attentive. He listened closely and teared up when touched by something he'd heard or read. Physically restless, he could draw on deep pools of stillness when writing and reading. Andre was a superb reader; his essay on his own long-evolving comprehension of Hemingway's "In Another Country" is one of the very best I have ever seen on that thoroughly scrutinized writer.

He had no want of ambition, but always rejoiced when some friend's good work got its due. And he took none of his own hard-won success for granted. He loved the ideals of the soldier—courage, comradeship, endurance, self-denial—but in the end the pictures on his wall were of Dorothy Day and Gandhi.

I miss my friend. I miss hearing that laugh explode from him like a blast from the mouth of a mine. I miss being called Silent Death. I miss the quiet and serious times, talking about our families, our work, something good we'd read and wanted the other to read. I miss hearing him read his stories and riff on the questions afterwards. I miss drinking with him and being needled by him and fishing with him and watching him deftly filet our catch with the Marine K-Bar knife he kept so deadly sharp, honing the blade on an oiled whetstone at the kitchen table with his friends and family all around, drinking, talking, laughing.

Note on the Type

The typography is a fusion of eighteenth- and twentieth-century fonts (Caslon and *Kaufmann*). William Caslon (1693-1766) was an influential force in the advancement of British typography, challenging Dutch domination of the type market during the period. His work with arabic, italic, and roman fonts are felt in the modern rendering of the classic that reshaped typesetting and document design in Europe and pre-/post-revolutionary America. Max Kaufmann's 1936 type creation uses smooth lines to add a powerful warmth to the work's titles. This combination gives the text an academic formality while capturing the essays' depth and creativity as the writers explore the rich world of Andre Dubus.

Cover and book design by **Gary Mills**

Gary Mills is Assistant Professor of English at the United States Air Force Academy. He is design director for *War Literature & the Arts: An International Journal of the Humanities.*